"Because poetry is about life — the good, the tragic, the shallow, and the deep. It is bone and marrow in our world. It erupts from our deepest loves, fears, ponderings, and pain, spilling out in the metaphors of life." — Vicki Wilke

"Writing about cancer is healing…. We need to touch [cancer] back, acknowledge it, and continue to love in the face of the pain, challenge, and loss we may experience." — Courtney Putnam

"I found that cancer produces all kinds of feelings, images, moods, and creative feelings. Maintaining a healthy, positive outlook calls upon all of one's creativity and resiliency." — Dennis A. Norlin

"There is the relief of writing, of scribbling out one's feelings onto paper, even if no one else ever sees those writings." — Jennifer Freed

"Why write poetry about cancer? Why not? It's got the two great themes — love and death. Plus, it helped me to get through those last two years, knowing that every moment we still had was a cherished moment. I didn't want to forget anything." — Megan Willome

"I don't think so much about writing about cancer in particular, but I think a lot about writing to help others, to pass along some of my experience and [my son's] so that someone else who is suffering or grieving might feel a little less alone in their circumstance." — Micah Chatterton

"In short, writing about cancer facilitates healing." — J. Anna Michaelis

"When I see my niece sick, or when I go to the funeral of a four-year-old boy who the week before loved SpongeBob and dinosaurs and suffered more than anyone should ever have to fathom — I feel helpless. Writing poems is one of the (small) ways in which I try to spread awareness of childhood cancer." — Amy Marengo

"Writing about cancer for me, and one hopes for the reader, is a means of reducing its power." — Philip Cate Huckins

"I have always used my writing to make sense of what I am experiencing in my life and to reach out to others in the slim hope of making a deep momentary connection." — Gail Rudd Entrekin

"[Writing] poetry helps a physician understand the emotional and physical impact cancer has on patients by asking relevant questions." — John Manesis, M.D.

"Writing about cancer or disease and death in poetic form is a reminder of our own mortality and illustrates the grace some people show facing it. It's important to celebrate the lives of people who inspire us with their courage. Also, it makes it harder to be petty in the face of their examples." — Bill Carpenter

"I have had cancer and so have three of my sisters, numerous friends, and acquaintances. It's terribly common but also frightening and mysterious. I want to do my tiny bit to put it into words." — Mara Faulkner, OSB

"Writing is often an attempt to find or create meaning in life events and to share with others. It's a human necessity to do this in one way or another. With a disease like cancer, which can be so lonely and terrifying, it's important to reach out and share, so others can maybe feel less alone." — Janet S. Meury

"I feel it's my job, my duty, as a poet to remember people [who've died from cancer]. As a human being, I just couldn't let these people go without somehow memorializing them. I loved them all and miss them greatly." — Larry Schug

"Poetry is cathartic and allows me to process and distill emotional events into a deeper, richer understanding of myself. When I weave together just the right words, or read poems that resonate with my own experience, it pulls back a veil and allows me to glimpse the beautiful golden web that connects us all together." — Susan Bernardo

the cancer poetry project 2

the cancer poetry project 2

more poems by cancer patients
and those who love them

EDITED BY KARIN B. MILLER

Tasora

Tasora Books, Minneapolis

Library of Congress Cataloging-in-Publications Data
The cancer poetry project 2 : more poems by cancer patients and those who love them / edited by Karin B. Miller

  p. cm.
  ISBN 978-1-934690-65-9
    1. Cancer patients' writings, American and Canadian. 2. Medical personnel, Writings of, American. 3. Cancer-Patients-Family relationships—Poetry. 4. American poetry—21st century. 5. Cancer—Patients—Poetry. 1. Miller, Karin B., 1964-

First Tasora Books Printing: April 2013
Printed in the United States of America

Cover design by Mike Schacherer
Book design by Brent Kastler

Permissions and acknowledgement for previous published work on page 274.

Tasora

Tasora Books
Distributed by Itasca Books Distribution
5120 Cedar Lake Rd.
Minneapolis, MN 55416

To Thom, who inspired *The Cancer Poetry Project,*
and to Gabi, Joey, and Mia. All my love.

ACKNOWLEDGEMENTS

Many people have believed in and supported *The Cancer Poetry Project* over the years. I offer my heartfelt thanks to all of them. The list below is hardly exhaustive, but it is a start.

• Thank you to every poet who has submitted a poem — whether or not your poem was selected. The task of selecting approximately 140 poems for each book was unbelievably challenging, not only because we received more than one thousand submissions for each book, but because the poetry was so strong, so moving, so breathtaking. Thank you for sharing it.

• Thank you, Mike Schacherer. Like last time, your vivid and hopeful cover is perfect. Thank you for your creativity, your endless design ideas, and your many generous hours.

• Thank you, Brent Kastler. You've been participating in the success of *The Cancer Poetry Project* since long before the first book even saw publication with your beautifully designed posters. This time around, thank you for the design of the book's interior, your attention to detail, and the many, many hours the actual work has required.

• Thank you to *The Cancer Poetry Project's* many cheerleaders — friends, writers, and colleagues — including Samantha Albert, Ultra-Sounds.org; Kristin Anderson, KA Comedy; Nadine Babu, Babu Social Networks; Janice Bednar; author Sharon Bray, Writing Through Cancer; Tami Cabrera, Muddy Paws Cheesecake; Mary Divine, *Pioneer Press;* J. Marie Fieger, Nemer Fieger; Joel Hoekstra, Refresh Content; Pamela McComas, Topeka High School; Kim Ode, *Star Tribune;* Rich Parrish, Cancer Education; Tara Parker-Pope, *The New York Times;* Stacy Pearson, The Blogunteer; Kyle Potvin, Prickly Pear Poetry Project; Saranne Rothberg, The ComedyCures Foundation; Sarah Watkins; Kamy Wicoff, SheWrites.com; Rebecca Wilson, World Cancer Day Awareness Night; Cathy Wood, Shawnee Mission South High School; and so many more. Thank you!

• Thank you, Nicole Baxter. I know I can count on Bookmobile to create high-quality books — every time. You guys are amazing.

- Thank you, Mark Jung, Itasca Books Distribution, for your counsel and fantastic work over many years.

- Thank you, Kickstarter supporters! Your financial support has been crucial in making this book possible. I hope the resulting volume is worthy of your faith in the project. I offer my special thanks to Solomon Cohen, president, Lines of Hope for Cancer; William Flexner for his gift to honor the dedicated work of Cornucopia Cancer Support Center in Durham, North Carolina; Linda Sedgewick to support Sarah Torrey, her sister-in-law and *Cancer Poetry Project* poet; and Felice Zwas.

- Thank you to my dear college friends: Ann, Carol, Kris, Laurie, Marie, Mary, Melissa, Nancy, Robin, and Sonja. I know I can always look to any of you for wise counsel, kindness, and a great story that will make me laugh out loud. Our annual summer gatherings continue to inspire.

- A tremendous thanks to you, Dad and Mom. Your unflagging confidence in me has meant and continues to mean my successes always begin with you. I love you so much.

- Thank you to my contributing editors, especially my mom, Joy Bumgardner, a children's book author, poet and creative writing teacher; and my sister, Gaye Guyton, an educator extraordinaire.

- Thanks too to the rest of my extended family — in-laws too! Your support means the world!

- Gabi, Mia, and Joey: Here's the world's biggest hug of thanks. Thank you for Gabi's awesome Kickstarter video, your many good ideas, and your understanding of the many, many hours I have spent working to create this book.

- Most especially, thank you, Thom, my dear husband of twenty-one years — and counting. Your cancer experience inspired both my poetry and *The Cancer Poetry Project*. I thank God that you are here — with me, with our family. Thank you for your strong belief in me, my work, and this work in particular. You're the best.

KARIN B. MILLER, editor

CONTENTS

POEMS BY CANCER PATIENTS

POEMS BY SPOUSES, PARTNERS, AND LOVERS

POEMS BY FRIENDS AND HEALTH ADVISORS

* Selected winner in its category, i.e. Poems by Cancer Patients; Poems by Spouses, Partners, and Lovers; etc.

** Selected honorable mention in its category, i.e. Poems by Cancer Patients; Poems by Spouses, Partners, and Lovers; etc.

Poems by theme

COPING AND PERSEVERANCE

DENIAL

DIAGNOSIS

FACING DEATH

FEAR AND DESPERATION

The Cancer Poetry Project 2

GRIEF AND LOSS

HOPE AND JOY

HUMOR

LOVE

The Cancer Poetry Project 2

Hope is the thing with feathers —
That perches in the soul —
And sings the tune without the words —
And never stops — at all —
—*Emily Dickinson*

The inspiration for the cover of *The Cancer Poetry Project,* volume one, was "Farewell to Hair" by first-time poet Terri Hanson, who imagined baby birds "sleeping in my hair" after losing her hair during chemo. Her moving poem sparked the hopeful image of three blue eggs in a spare nest, drawing countless readers to pick up the book.

This time around, I was challenged by the idea of a cover — the books' brilliant cover designer, Mike Schacherer, can testify to that after I sent him in several different directions.

Then one day, thinking about that hopeful first cover, I searched for the word "bird" in the new book and discovered that many of our poets had referenced birds — not just blackbirds, bluebirds, chickadees, hummingbirds, and songbirds, but a Hummingbird guitar, a "flipped bird," "masks shaped like birds' beaks," "a birdlike chest," and many more. *Voila!* Here was our new spark — and one that was tied to and continued the promise of the first book. Mike than aptly suggested a hummingbird for the cover — in various Native American cultures, a hummingbird symbolizes life, joy, and accomplishing the impossible: perfect.

———

Fifteen years ago, my husband, Thom, was diagnosed with testicular cancer. We were devastated, but followed the recommended protocol of surgeries and chemotherapy, gathered our loved ones around us, and asked for prayers. Thankfully, Thom has been cancer free since 1998.

At the time of his cancer, I was pregnant. Three weeks after his final surgery, I delivered our daughter, Gabrielle Hope. Photographs of the two baldies — our darling baby and Thom from chemo — are both joyful and poignant. During and after this emotional roller coaster, I wrote poetry — fearful, angry, humorous, helpless, and, ultimately, triumphant.

One morning, when Gabi was six months old, I awoke with the idea of *The Cancer Poetry Project.* The details came to me like a calling: I wasn't even sure other people wrote cancer-themed poetry, but I was enthused and determined to create a national anthology.

Getting started

Dreaming up the idea, however, was far simpler than actually achieving it. After nearly a year of networking with myriad cancer organizations, I launched the project on a shoestring budget, sent out dozens of media kits, and mailed hundreds of flyers to cancer treatment centers and universities.

Soon, poems began trickling in, and a few weeks before the deadline, I was receiving nearly one hundred poems a week. Yet initial giddiness at the huge response quickly turned bittersweet at the realization of just how many of us are affected by cancer and how great the need was for this anthology.

Today, I'm thrilled to be the editor of both books: *The Cancer Poetry Project* and *The Cancer Poetry Project 2*. This second volume, like the first, features approximately 140 remarkable poems, thoughtfully selected from more than one thousand submissions. The poems are written by cancer patients and survivors, spouses and partners, family members and friends, doctors and nurses, and others. Poets are widely published, first-timers, and every degree in between. They range in age from seven to eighty-three. And their unique perspectives and life experiences combine to make a rich collection of poems. The diversity is on purpose: My mission from the beginning has been to create a book of poetry in which anyone affected by cancer would find solace and understanding.

How to read this book

If you're a patient, likely the poems by cancer patients and survivors will ring most true for you. If you're the significant other of a cancer patient, turn first to the chapter written by spouses, partners and lovers. You get the idea — not that poems from any chapter won't resonate with you. It's just that the writers of each chapter bring that perspective to their poems. Be sure, too, to check out the second contents section in which poems are categorized — so you can find, or avoid, poems by theme.

This is not an anthology you're likely to read in one sitting, but a book you'll pick up again and again — a book that may inspire you to write your own poetry (see "Writing Poetry," page 271).

When Thom was diagnosed with cancer, I couldn't imagine more terrible news. And yet our experience also brought an incredible outpouring of love from wonderful friends and family members, and it inspired *The Cancer Poetry Project*. I hope *The Cancer Poetry Project 2* is one of the good things you find on your cancer journey.

KARIN B. MILLER

POEMS BY CANCER PATIENTS

AFTER THE 34TH MRI

by Geo Staley

Marie and I sit in the examining room,
Again.
She says optimistic things:
> *It'll be fine. You've done so well.*
I nod in agreement.
> I have done well. And I'm here.

We wait.
I say, *We can't say we're optimistic. We
> have to believe it.*
She doesn't hesitate, she says, *I do.*
I say, *I do.*
As we wait for the door to open.

---

*After enduring brain cancer and its treatment — surgery, monthly
hospitalizations for a year, and chemotherapy for two additional years —
Geo Staley, sixty-one, is "on the planet (with no growth in the remains of the
tumor for eight years) and thankful for it," he says. "After the 34th MRI' catches
a moment in our adventure with cancer."*

Staley has two chapbooks: Where Orphans Live *(2003) and* Ready for
Any Nuance *(2011), both by FinishingLine Press. His poetry has been featured
in numerous literary magazines, including* Blue Stem, Evening Street Review,
and Main Street Rag. *His nonfiction has appeared in such diverse publications
as* The Journal of Thought, USA Today Magazine, *and* Momentum.

*Staley is retired from twenty-five years of teaching writing and literature at
Portland Community College. He also taught in New England, Appalachia and
on the Rosebud Sioux Indian Reservation. He now watches and learns from his
six-year-old "grandboy."*

ALPHA-BET

by Susan Martell Huebner

I write to tell my Christmas friends
the usual newsy update
breast cancer's gone
I mean to say

But the letter *r* slips
downstream
a silver minnow
and leaves me with the growl of *beast*
that paces beneath my startled pen
upon the page's four-cornered cage

beast
rattles the door and threatens the hinges
until the letter *s* shakes loose
by pounding *beat* of quaking heart

when all at once
a feather sigh of *a* floats down
an *ah* of breath released

deep in winter's throat
a sudden filling
a flutter of light
my body thrums with choirs of joy.

Susan Martell Huebner, sixty-four, says she couldn't not *write about her experience with breast cancer. This poem stems from both making words from other words and betting on herself "to heal without the chemo," which her body couldn't tolerate. She is a four-year survivor.*

Huebner's poetry has been featured in Free Verse, Museletter, Aroostook Review *and other literary publications. She teaches writing and reading at Milwaukee Area Technical College.*

She and her husband live in Waukesha County, Wisconsin, and have four grandsons and one granddaughter — "the first baby girl in our family in thirty-five years!" They also have three cats, one of which enjoys sitting in Huebner's lap as she writes and dipping a paw into her coffee.

AWARENESS

by Lisa S. Lutwyche

As if October didn't already bring it all back.
The chill, the falling,
tasting death on my tongue
      with woodsmoke.

Pink doesn't go with all the browns, reds
and yellows, but they mean well.
Their annual alert will save someone, somewhere.

Recovering, I watched the trees that autumn.
Their brilliant colors were a bright rapture,
settling around their feet like a celebration.

If only I could have shed my breast
the way a tree slips her leaves.
A sign, a tremor, and then she rests.

She sleeps through the cold, harsh nights,
Confident she will wake with the flowers.
No surgeon's knife for her, no pain, no terror.
      The letting go so easy.

"I write because I have something inside of me that will not leave me alone until I free it," says Lisa S. Lutwyche, fifty-seven. *"Breast cancer had such an overwhelming influence on how I thought about my life forever after, that I suppose it isn't surprising to find myself writing about it."*

Poems, prose, and plays by Lutwyche, a Pushcart Prize nominee, have appeared in numerous literary magazines and anthologies, including Pitkin Review, Falklands War Poetry, *and* Mad Poets Review.

Following an abusive marriage and debilitating divorce, Lutwyche was laid off from her job in the midst of her cancer treatments. While she still has not fully recovered financially from paying medical bills, she and her second husband "live in the woods of Chester County, Pennsylvania, with our half dozen rescued cats." She works three jobs and has just completed her Master of Fine Arts degree in creative writing at Goddard College.

BATTLE ON THE BEACH

by Stephen J. Kudless

How many days, how many nights
Have I sat alone in the dark and waited,
At the water's edge,
For you, who devoured my mother, to return,
This time for me?
Did I believe that you would be captured
Chained, restrained — kept away?
At times, I pretended that you did not exist,
That you were a forgotten ghost or superstition,
A creature of others' imaginations
(And even my own)
Like a monster in the deep,
A shark in grainy, water photos,
Not frightening, a Hollywood fiction.

I put it off,
Thinking about you,
Turning fear into folly and foolishness.
I had better things to do,
More important, more timely, more true.
I waded in rejected memories up to my knees,
And, bolder still, up to my waist and beyond.
The cries of others floated over my head,
Unheeded, unwanted — intrusions to the calm.

Then, on a pleasant day, unexpected,
You returned to tear at me
And to bring me below.

Face to face, eye to eye
I can feel your teeth, your pulling, and your determination.

Can you feel mine?

Stephen J. Kudless is a poet and playwright whose mother died of cancer in 1989. In January 2012, he discovered, while submitting for a routine hernia repair, that he instead had a large liposacrcoma. Fortunately, it was successfully removed and, following radiation therapy, he remains cancer free.

"I wrote this poem, in a sense, to establish that I am the same person now that I was before the cancer came to me," he says, adding that he'd feel the same even if the surgery hadn't been as successful.

Kudless has had numerous poems in publications and anthologies, including The Country and Abroad, Light: The Journal of Light Verse, *and* The New York Times. *Two of his plays,* How Fish Breathe *and* Beds, *were produced in off-off Broadway venues, and he is currently working on a new play,* Altar Boys.

In September 2011 he retired from his post as an instructor in the English department of Touro College, New York City. He and his wife of forty-eight years maintain residences in both Staten Island and Manhattan. "We like to visit our grandchildren, Ryan and Lindsey, as often as possible. Life is good."

THE BREAST AND THE BRIGHTEST
I exist as I am, that is enough. — Walt Whitman

by Cindy Hochmann

My breasts, size 34B, are an issue now. Once upon a time they were quiet and hung to hemselves, cute and unassuming behind tanks and halters. Now they are the subject of sinister sonograms and perplexing path reports, to say nothing of my ongoing morbid speculation. You would think they were pendulous.

They used to be precious and loved, now I treat them like bastard children, the terrible twos, troublemakers, twins gone bad, truly out of hand, spitting pureed peas at Mommy, burning their training bras, defying their curfews, smoking Virginia Slims (and Lord knows what else) on the corner with their lowlife friends. Where did I go wrong?

Old boyfriends call, concerned: "But are they still pink? Are they still nubile? Do they still stand on ceremony, rise to the occasion, and come when called?" Nostalgia sets in like rigormortis, but I respond in a wholly Whitmanesque way: They exist as they are, that is enough.

Next they will be the hot topic of a filibuster (pun intended) on the Senate floor. Even with 250,000 miles on them and graffitied beyond recognition, they deserve to be signed into law.

This is in memory of David Halberstam. Not only did I rip off the title of his magnificent book for use in my less-than-magnificent poem.

But I did it in such a cheap and tawdry way.

A lifelong hypochondriac, Cindy Hochmann, fifty-five, found her breast cancer diagnosis to be "my worst nightmare." Despite that, her saucy writing style shines through her cancer-related poems. "My poetry tends to be a bit on the satirical side, and I suppose this was my fearful but optimistic way of dealing with the dreadful diagnosis.

"As poets, we write what we know," she continues. "Those of us who have experienced it have different takes on it, depending on our mindsets. Poetry is a fine way of gaining control over our demons, whether they be physical or emotional."

Hochmann's writings have been included in The New York Quarterly, The Stray Branch, *and* Möbius, The Poetry Magazine, *plus other journals. Her book reviews have appeared in* Pedestal Magazine, Pirene's Fountain, Home Planet News, *and others. Her chapbook,* The Carcinogenic Bride, *includes several poems about cancer.*

Hochmann works as a legal assistant, a freelance proofreader, editor of First Literary Review - East, *and a book reviewer. She lives in Sheepshead Bay, Brooklyn, and is a proud New Yorker. Her newest venture is studying Russian language and culture.*

BREAST IMAGING

by Ann Cefola

In the bluest of rooms, I am awash in x-ray white.
My body's on lease to strangers:

Wrapped in paper, I mourn my lost topography,
my front yard with its swings and sand box.

Around one breast a radiologist rolls metal in gel.
Traveling this ultrasound moonscape,

I see black pools pulse like tar pits.
She reassures, just cysts.

Poured into warm cotton held close,
my chaste white communicants

return to their warm-scented knit,
eyes like pink crocuses in snow,

roots delicate and lacey in red earth,
my certain garden, my creamy whole.

———

Ann Cefola, fifty-five, works as a communications professional. It's not surprising then that she has given some thought to why she writes poetry. "Poetry especially tells us not only how to survive but how to thrive in the face of enormous personal challenge," she says. "In a compact space, between lyrical images, something escapes that feels a little divine."

Cefola's previously published works have appeared in Sugaring *(Dancing Girl Press),* St. Agnes, Pink-Slipped *(Kattywompus Press), and the translation* Hence This Cradle *(Seismicity Editions).*

As for her hobbies, Cefola is "crazy in love with pit bull-type dogs," and she advocates for shelter reforms in New York City.

BREATHING

by Joanne E. Cooper

She asked me to breathe into her stethoscope,
Deep breaths, in, out.
Suddenly Kim breathes with me,
then Jake, in out,
my oncologist, laughing.
A circle of breathing in that tiny white room,
breathing like humans do.
Each breathing alone, or
so we think.

---

*To her first chemo session, Joanne E. Cooper's husband, Jake, and daughter Kim
accompanied her. Their experience together sparked this poem. "Poetry helps you
feel less alone in what can be a horrendous process," Cooper says. "You see this
reflected in my poem — feeling alone and yet not alone. I was surrounded by my
competent doctor and my loving daughter and husband."*

*While Cooper is a professor emeritus of the University of Hawaii with five
published books and many scholarly articles, this is her first published poem.
"My poems helped me survive [my colon cancer], as did the poems in the first
volume of* The Cancer Poetry Project."

*Cooper lives in Honolulu, Hawaii, and has a loving, supportive husband,
two daughters and four grandchildren, plus a circle of loving friends and a
wonderful caring church. She says, "All helped me through this ordeal."*

CHAYOTE FRUIT

by Kyle Potvin

On a beach in Brazil,
sipping Caipirinhas,
sweet and sour slipping
down my throat,
it's all I can do
not to stare at breasts,
round and perfect
like those on last night's
samba dancers.

On the streets,
the produce stalls are vibrant
with cabbages and beets,
rutabagas and tomatoes.
My fingers explore
each sphere.

A chayote fruit with bumpy skin
sends my mind where
it shouldn't go
and I draw my hand
to my chest.

At the next stall,
a man with a machete
cleaves a coconut,
removes a useless piece,
offers me milk
from its shell.

Kyle Potvin, forty-seven, was diagnosed with breast cancer when her children were four and six years old. While she remains in remission, every year before her annual mammogram, she grows anxious. "Right before one annual visit, I went to Rio de Janeiro for work," she says. "The images of the samba dancers, the produce-filled market and the machete all collided with my apprehension about the visit to form 'Chayote Fruit.'"

Potvin was so moved by reading and writing poetry during her illness that she and poet Tammi Truax, who lost her husband to cancer, founded The Prickly Pear Poetry Project in 2008. "We hold poetry workshops and readings at oncology clinics, churches, etcetera for anyone who has been touched by cancer. Each session is so incredibly moving."

Potvin's poetry has appeared in Measure, JAMA, Literary Mama, The New York Times' *"Well" blog, and other publications. She was named a finalist for the 2008 Howard Nemerov Sonnet Award. She is president of the Poetry Society of New Hampshire and helps coordinate the Robert Frost Farm's Hyla Brook Reading Series. Her first poetry collection is* Sound Travels on Water *(Finishing Line Press, 2012).*

Potvin is principal of a public relations firm. She lives in Derry, New Hampshire, with her husband and two sons.

ELEGY FOR THAT GIRL IN THE POLKA DOT BRA

Courage is no good:
It means not scaring others. Being brave
Lets no one off the grave.
Death is no different whined at than withstood.

Philip Larkin

by Sarah Torrey

Snapshot caught the far away look

— patio, brick heat, sleeveless tee,
clapboards peeling, garage door
part way up, barrels half full —

her head cocked to the side and leaning
on her hand on a thin arm, freckled; bald,
bald like an old man bald, bald like an eagle bald,
like an egg, like a cue ball, like a skull revealed.

I liked the look, honestly, the raw tenderness
and big hoops, standard issue, the look in her eye.

I miss her; who stood out in the dusk yard, shirtless,
wore a polka dot bra and held an apple, unbitten
right where the breast would soon not be,
swollen face from steroids, held it smiling for the photo
(Hold that!) looked at the camera with a *Fuck you, take it!*
now that it's November and the goose bumps
and the ho hum.

That part was easy in a way, a ride — numbered ticket
from a colored roll and she just got on and watched
the tree tops and the cars parked and the sani-cans
all in a row and round and round and up and down
it's not a choice to watch the world rise up, recede,

a little nausea, but not so bad, until the car slows,
you climb off, not a choice so much.
The music just stops.

She marched in that parade with torches
where women wore pink banners
like they'd won something.

I dare not miss her and her bald
nerve and the clear eye, far away eye,
all sheer and glowing lack of future, regrets
bundled with twine behind the wood pile, carrot greens
feathering up in raised beds, with yellow
beets, sage, apple mint invading.

I do not really miss her. I do not miss her.
I dare not.

———————

*Before being diagnosed with stage-three breast cancer just over five years ago,
Sarah Torrey, fifty-four, never had written poetry. "I had to begin, simply,"
she says. "I tried hard to deny the 'blood jet' quality of its arrival, a relentless
insistence to be heard. It took quite a while to allow even myself to hear it, let
alone to write it, and share it with others." This is her first published poem.*

*"Until I wrote this poem, I didn't realize how much I missed the me who
had to go through all of the above and manage it with considerable grace,"
she says. "Figuring out how to live my daily life now with some fraction of the
clarity and intensity of that time turns out to be much harder."*

*Torrey is a psychotherapist in Providence, Rhode Island. Since her cancer
treatment, she says, "I feel I am doing the best work I've ever done with the
people who find me, who range from very young to adult."*

*She lives with her husband of almost twenty years and two teenage sons in a
two-hundred-and-fifty-year-old farmhouse. They have five chickens, two dogs,
and a huge vegetable garden. Torrey continues to write poetry, "though not as
much and not all about cancer and death anymore." Now she finds herself
writing about her chickens.*

FEDEX

by Clinton B. Campbell

When it comes it's pointed and sharp
    a knife unsheathed
    in a package not ordered.
We hope it's the neighbor's.
Or a mistake on the label, but today,
it was delivered by Federal Express.

This morning they brought
the "C" word into our house.
We signed the release
then endorsed our denial.
The attached yellow tag,
"Bad news in your gene pool,"
says one of us will wane
in less that a month, or suffer
for years with too little rest.

No one mentions that word
not even in whispers.
We swallow it down
with our eggs and burnt toast,
then smile the lie
with everyday small talk.
We say things are fine… but,
today it was delivered Federal Express.

Seated at his desk for three days without writing a word, Clinton B. Campbell,
seventy-seven, watched a FedEx driver deliver an envelope to his next door
neighbors. He thought, "what if?" and wrote this denial-themed poem. "In a
crisis, the first emotion we use to deal with is denial," he says. Campbell wanted
the poem's readers to see denial as the first step and a normal one toward recovery.

"FedEx" won the Carol M. Wimberg Memorial Award from the
New Jersey Poetry Society and was published in A String of Colored Beads,
NJPS Anthology 2006.

Campbell's poetry has appeared in MARGIE, California Quarterly,
Passager *and* The Journal of New Jersey Poets. *His work also has appeared in*
The Cancer Poetry Project, *volume one, and his poem, "My Veteran's Day*
Prayer," was entered into the Congressional Record. *Campbell moved from*
New Jersey twelve years ago, and he now lives in Beaufort, South Carolina, with
his wife, photographer and poet Karen M. Peluso.

GRACE

by Sarah Knorr

In the raku kiln of cancer
superheated clay grows luminous,
fluid of form. No longer day-drab
the body — translucent —
is lit from within.

The world looks different every after.
Even when the furnace cools,
the vessel gleams through the ash —
oxidized, reduced and refined;
restored to its elemental grace.

---

*Sarah Knorr, fifty-seven, has "personally danced four times with cancer,"
beginning with Hodgkins disease, twice, in her early thirties, then skin cancer in
her late thirties, and thyroid cancer in her fifties. "I remain so grateful that all
four times, we discovered the cancer in time to address it effectively," she says.*

*Knorr writes poetry to make sense of things and to distill meaning. "This
poem," she says, "is about the reductive nature of many cancers and treatments,
the removal of body parts and privacy, the stripping away and the letting go
until that fierce remainder at the core shines out unimpeded."*

Her poetry, fiction and non-fiction have appeared in Ashe Journal, Earth's
Daughters, Tough Times Companion, *and the anthology* Sisters Singing,
among others.

*Knorr has worked in human services and advocacy throughout her life. She
now savors "life with my beloved husband of many years, our intrepid children,
and our granddaughter, whose attention to wonder reminds us of the magic in
any given roadside pebble." She lives in Verona, Virginia.*

HAMMAM IN OUARZAZATE, MOROCCO

by Natalie Olsen

This is the coming-out party
for my scarred breast, I realize
in the steamy room full of naked
Muslim women, some who'd show
only their eyes on the street.
Friendly now and curious,
leaning against the walls or lying down,
they watch me pretend that
sweating on a stone floor
and smearing myself with brown
molasses-like stuff is how
I often spend an afternoon.

"Lie down, please," the woman who'll scrub me says.
"B'shuay, min fadlak," I tell her,
pointing to my dented breast,
as if she hadn't seen the surgeon's ragged seam.
Her brown breasts with quarter-sized nipples
bob over me as she scrapes off dead skin
in spaghetti strips with her sandpaper sponge
but goes tenderly over my scars as I'd asked.
She pours hot water over me from buckets,
rubs, turns me over and scrubs,
washes my body, shampoos my hair,
then rubs my back while singing Berber lullabies
that echo in the steamy stone-walled room.

Natalie Olsen, seventy-three, was diagnosed with breast cancer in 2005.
After a trip to Morocco, she wrote this poem describing her visit to a hammam,
or steam bath.

Olsen's poetry has been heard on National Public Radio and has appeared
in Seattle's Poetry on the Buses Project, literary journals and anthologies,
including The Cancer Poetry Project, *volume one.*

Olsen is a fiber artist whose weaving studio is on Whidbey Island,
north of Seattle, where she lives with her husband of fifty years. Pink is not her
favorite color.

HAVE YOU

by Gwendolyn Morgan

A few of the 10,000 things people said to her while she was receiving chemotherapy:

Stay positive — that is the most important thing — you gotta stay positive, keep smiling.
What kind? what stage? Oh, my sister-in-law had that at stage three and she's doing great; she had to give up smoking and drinking, but that's been ten years ago.
God must be really telling you to slow down.
Dr. Yes has a vegetarian ayurvedic diet that has been proven to cure cancer.
Have you taken some time for yourself?
Is there a history of cancer in your family?
Your hair looks cute short.
Are you juicing your fruits and veggies? Studies show that an alkaline and vegetarian diet is effective in preventing most cancers.
You're so young and fit — this will be behind you before you know it.
If there is anything you need, just let us know…anything at all.
I think of people who get cancer have anger — not people who are positive like you.
What kind? Oh, my friend had that fifteen years ago and she's living in Japan now.
You look like a Buddhist monk, so serene.
Do you ever read the Bible? I've been thinking of some scripture passages for you.
I can't believe it — now, I'm freaking out — you are an athlete, you eat fabulously, you have a great life, I mean, anyone could get it; maybe I need to go in for a checkup.
May you find the wisdom to listen to your illness.
I'm going to Brazil to meet John of God, I'll take your photo with me and ask for healing.
Have you been learning a lot about yourself?
Of all the people I know, you have the emotional and spiritual strength to do this.

Have you had your water pH checked? Has anyone checked your house for toxins?

Have you read Dr. Bernie Siegel?

Forgiveness is a choice. Forgiveness is a gift you give yourself. Forgiveness equates with freedom from the shackles of anger and resentment. You should know that.

F — k!

If you have enough faith, you can beat this, I know it.

Where did you grow up? There are really high incidences of cancer in California.

Life doesn't happen to you, life happens for you.

Are you, like, really depressed?

There is evidence showing that eating four tablespoons of cooked asparagus a day has shown to cure some types of cancer.

Anyway, have you checked into clinical studies? There is no profit in curing cancer.

I'll keep you in my thoughts and prayers.

What is it like to lose your hair? I mean, you had beautiful hair.

They think that black-capped chickadees have cancer now. There are studies showing unusual beak formations, so the songbirds cannot even eat sunflower seeds.

Is there a history of pain in your family?

You have a wellspring of spiritual strength to draw on, more so than anyone I know.

You are tough, we can do this.

Gwendolyn Morgan, forty-nine, was moved to write "Have You" from her own, and others', cancer experiences with "well-intentioned family, friends, coworkers, and strangers, offering unsolicited advice and commentary."

With a Master of Fine Arts degree in creative writing from Goddard College and a Master of Divinity degree from San Francisco Theological Seminary, she has been a recipient of writing residencies at Artsmith, Caldera, and Soapstone. Morgan has poetry published in Calyx, Dakotah, Kalliope, *and other literary journals. She serves as an interfaith chaplain and manager of spiritual care at a medical center. Gwen and partner Judy share their Salmon Creek, Washington, home with Abbey Skye, a rescued Pembroke Welsh Corgi.*

HYMN TO A LOST BREAST

by Bonnie Mauer

Oh let it fly
let it fling
let it flip like a pancake in the air
let it sing: what is the song
of one breast flapping?

Send it soaring, a saucer into the autumn sky,
the sweet gum leaves laughing.
Make it a balloon, tie a string,
redyelloworange and one breast sailing.
Stuff it, paint pink roses,
call your reckless needles and pins.

Sew a pocket for Grandma's cards and canasta wins.
Make a purse for her lost buttons and peppermints.
Shape an instrument, pluck its nipple, play it,
squeeze it, heart its
concertina song and let it sing:

Oh I am gone
I am long
I am a lazy drift
of milkweed in the air,
daydream somewhere,
atoms returning to the stars.

Bonnie Maurer, sixty-three, was diagnosed with breast cancer at forty-nine and chose a ninety-five percent survival rate at the time with a mastectomy. She was awarded a Creative Renewal Fellowship from the Arts Council of Indianapolis and Lilly Endowment to compose a series of poems on breast cancer. Her poems have appeared in literary magazines and anthologies, including And Know This Place: Poetry of Indiana *and* The Cancer Poetry Project, *volume one. Finishing Line Press published* The Reconfigured Goddess: Poems of a Breast Cancer Survivor, *her book of breast cancer poems and corresponding art by Andrea Eberbach, award-winning artist and book designer. The 2013 release is sponsored by the Heroes Foundation, which serves the cancer community in Indianapolis.*

Maurer works as a copy editor for the Indianapolis Business Journal, *as a poet for Arts for Learning, and as an Ai Chi (aquatic flowing energy) instructor.*

I NEED SOME RITUAL

by Jamie L. Steckelberg

The Apache embrace
White Painted Woman, brush
Her body with cornmeal
And clay, massage her changing
Form. She blesses
Them with pollen, gives thanks
In the four directions, and runs
Toward the sunrise.

No one marked the
Official budding
Of my breasts
That arrived.
My mother took
Me to Younkers
For the move from
The half shirt
With cartoons
to the A cup.

I need some form of ritual
To let them go, to grieve
My girls. Wave them with sage,
Anoint them with oil,
Slick them with love.
Cup them now in your hand,
Gently caress bruised
flesh and bloody marks.
Soothe my scars, watch the sun
rise, let your tongue kindle and unearth
Desires. Tears soften their anger.
Tell them "Go in love,"
"Go in love."

Jamie L. Steckelberg, forty-seven, was diagnosed with breast cancer in 2009. She wrote this poem because "I felt at a loss to create some kind of physical ritual around the actual act of a bilateral mastectomy." This was the first time after receiving her bachelor's degree that she felt brave enough to submit a poem for publication.

Shortly after completing chemotherapy treatment, she attended a breast cancer recovery retreat where she learned how to zipline. She also attended an Amherst Writers and Artists conference to become a writing facilitator for cancer groups and currently leads a group called Write to Heal for Gilda's Club in Middleton, Wisconsin.

Steckelberg lives in Madison, Wisconsin, with her partner, Shaheen; their six-year-old daughter, Josie; plus, two cats, a dog, and a gecko. She teaches English at Madison College.

INFUSION FRIDAYS

by Terry Godbey

Each week I'm led off
to the clinic for my infusion,
as if I'll be handed a steaming,
fragrant cup of pleasure.
My wig's a supercranial prosthesis,
and I'm not a yacht but have my own port,
below my clavicle, so the poison
can go straight to my heart.
The chemo room is nothing
like the ocean
or even a river;
it's a murky swimming hole
with snakes and gators and turtles
— snap, snap, snap go the nurses' gloves.
None of us can swim now.
We are seasick, reclining
in our deck chairs,
hoodwinked tourists
who pulled out the wrong tickets,
were spit out into a perilous land
where the healthy send postcards.
We can't escape
the punishing, fluorescent sun,
yet we are still cold,
wrapped in blankets,
lamenting our lots,
hopeless, tired, run aground.
Sometimes we talk,
but mostly we don't.
It seems rude to ask,
What kind have you got?

I have neither spinnaker nor jib,
but I'm trying to sail
my failing body
far, far away from here,
to a place where I can tread water
and see the bottom.

Terry Godbey, fifty-seven, says poetry helped her survive her battle with breast cancer. "It was oddly satisfying to write this poem about the misery and helplessness I felt during chemo treatments," she says. "At least I could control my words on the page." The poem was performed during The Pink Ribbon Project *at Orlando Repertory Theater in 2011 and was published in* The Florida Review *in 2012.*

Godbey has written three poetry collections: Flame *(2012);* Beauty Lessons, *winner of the 2009 Quercus Review Poetry Series Book Award; and* Behind Every Door, *winner of Slipstream's annual chapbook award in 2006. The winner of the Rita Dove Poetry Award in 2008, Godbey lives in Orlando, Florida, with her teenage son and works as a freelance writer and editor.*

IN THE OTHER ROOM

by Kelina Leeks

in the other room
sounds
utensils on plates
water at the kitchen sink

voices of the two
I love

only occasional words
of their conversation
meander their way
to me in the other room
only a few words
I understand
the rest of the letters
absorbed into the walls

but the sounds
the oven door opening
a chair being pulled out

laying here
on the couch
wondering if this is what it will sound like
when I am gone.

Kelina Leeks, forty-six, was diagnosed with stage-two, grade-three breast cancer in 2011. While she endured surgery, chemotherapy, radiation, and Herceptin therapy, she was only one month into treatment when she wrote this poem. "Writing takes the thoughts outside of me and leaves more space in my mind and heart to deal with the cancer and healing," she says. This is her first published poem.

Leeks has a master's degree in social work and has worked nearly all of her professional life in hospital-based social work, most recently with a traumatic brain injury team. She lives in Montreal, Quebec, with her husband, Daniel, and eighteen-year-old son, Nicholas.

JUST WHAT I NEEDED

by Arwen Kuttner

This box
delivered our wedding proofs.
Two years later
it held the pills —

bottles so large
they rolled on their sides
and small ones
that stood still within.

We bought an organizer
with compartments
for each time of day

And you counted
one by one,
my every pill
and stood by me
holding the glass of water
as I placed the bitter tablets
on my tongue.

So much of my healing came
from solitary walks
from meditation
from shouting obscenities
inside a closed car
or pulling sheets over my head.

But you pulled the sheet back
and handed me
love
just what I needed for that day.

Arwen Kuttner credits her husband for getting her through non-Hodgkins lymphoma at age twenty-six. "His constant, steady, unobtrusive presence was so vital to my recovery that I can't think about or imagine the experience without him there in the background," she says.

Poetry is her natural outlet. "When something big like cancer comes along, writing is my vehicle to explain and to heal," says Kuttner, now thirty-six. "Poetry brings you into the moment in a way that is different than prose."

Her published credits include a series of articles about cancer and spirituality at Aish.com, and her chapbook, Gathering Pieces. *She is also a blogger for Voices: Powerful Learning Practice.*

Kuttner teaches elementary school and lives in Englewood, New Jersey, with her husband and daughter.

LETTER WRITER

by Marcia Renée Goodman

All week I've tried to write a letter to my son
for he says he likes to see handwriting and envelope with a real stamp.
Out of habit I hesitate: a letter
is so different from an email, nowadays a letter
should say something profound or at least important.
And then too I worry about the paper's fragility,
how it's so easily lost, misplaced, gone in a flood and what if
he lost my letters and I had died,
would he walk around always searching
dusty corners for them?
There would be memory, I reassure myself, the memory of having opened
them and read them, which maybe matters more than what's in them.
After all, I remember those postcards my father
sent me from Rome, though not what he said,
how he filled every space, writing upside down and on the diagonal,
his desire to communicate bouncing off the page and into my upstate
New York dormitory that crazy summer.
I'd turn them in my hands, study the pictures, imagine
him traipsing over cobblestones alone.
I didn't notice then the text was always upbeat, funny, as if
he were never sad. That's the nature of the postcard, I suppose,
or the nature of how parents are with children sometimes.
But a letter can get out of control, ramble from pleasure to difficulty
before coming back. And how much
to tell a child who's just twenty-one about
how sometimes it's an act of courage to get out of bed in the morning
let alone put words down on paper.

Marcia Renée Goodman, fifty-eight, says the "desire of my adult children to know me as much as they possibly can" moved her to write this poem.

Goodman was diagnosed with ovarian cancer in 1998, has experienced multiple surgeries and bouts of chemotherapy, and today continues maintenance treatment.

"Cancer is a part of life and raises important feelings and questions," she says. "Writing about cancer is also a way of considering mortality; a felt sense of mortality is behind so many poems, one way or another."

Goodman has had poems, essays, and fiction published in journals and anthologies, including Writing on the Edge, The Jewish Women's Poetry Anthology, Box of Rocks, *and* The Cancer Poetry Project, *volume one.*

Goodman is a professor of English at Diablo Valley College in Pleasant Hill, California. She earned her Ph.D. in English Literature at University of California Berkeley and then settled in Berkeley, where, with her husband, she raised a family. She grew up in Brooklyn, New York.

THE LOST BREASTS

by Pat Riviere-Seel

They never nourished a child, never gave me pleasure, pleased only a few others. They were cherry tomatoes, not Beefsteak or Big Boy, nothing better about those breasts. If I wanted cleavage, I fenced them with underwire, lifted, and corralled them into padding. The nipples were pink, like a baby. My baby breasts were mostly an embarrassment. But I had grown comfortable with them. Small and still perky, they fit nicely into an "Almost A," fit my sports bra perfectly. They didn't bounce or bob when I ran. They didn't define me, or my sexuality. Six decades those songbird breasts rode on my chest. When I looked in the mirror after surgery at the flat plane of my torso, I marveled at the hunk of clay, a place to begin again, space that could become anything.

> freshly plowed earth
> morning frost on opened rows
> waiting for new life

Pat Riviere-Seel, sixty-three, teaches poetry at the University of North Carolina at Asheville, and says she took her own advice to students. "When the subject you're writing about is emotionally charged and close to the bone, try using a formal structure for your poem. It will force you to say things that might surprise you."

This poem is a haibun, which combines a prose poem and haiku. "I have to write about cancer," says this poet, who has reached her third year of remission from breast cancer. "Poetry says what prose cannot say — where there are no words, there is poetry."

A former newspaper journalist, Riviere-Seel has published two collections of poetry, No Turning Back Now *and* The Serial Killer's Daughter, *winner of the North Carolina Literary and Historical Society's Roanoke-Chowan Award. Riviere-Seel earned a Master of Fine Arts in poetry from Queens University of Charlotte, North Carolina. She is a fellow in the Hambidge Creative Residency Program.*

She has run three marathons and still enjoys running trails and racing. She lives in the beautiful Blue Ridge Mountains with her husband, Ed, and two spoiled cats. They share their land with black bears, wild turkeys, and other assorted wildlife.

MIRACLES

by Paul Hostovsky

Spiritual texts are the most boring books in the world.
None of them mentions a bicycle
or a Ferris wheel, or baseball, or sea lions, or ice cream.
They just lump them all together into "the world."
The "world of appearances." The "world of illusions."
You can walk through this world and not
believe it for a minute. You can get to the end of it
and not believe that either. The miracle is seeing
right through the world to another
world that's right here, right now.
But you have to let go of everything.
You have to let go of everything — you can
start by letting go of these words, just let them
go. Let them fall through the air, skim
your knee, spill to the floor. How to read these words
when they're lying on the floor face-down
like bodies? That is the seeming difficulty.
You can sit in a small room all alone with your body
and not believe it for a minute. You can
don the humble johnny that closes in the back,
and when the doctor comes in with his numbers
which are your numbers, you can
not believe them either. You can let them fall from his lips,
skim your ear, pool on the floor where your eyes
and his eyes have fallen. He won't
mention the bicycle, or the Ferris wheel which is
taking up a lot of room right now in the little
examining room where a sea lion has clambered up
onto the table and is barking, and the baseballs are flying,
and the vendors are hawking ice cream — because he can't
see them. He can't perform a miracle.

Paul Hostovsky, fifty-four, writes about "whatever occurs to me. So when
cancer occurred" — in his case, non-Hodgkins lymphoma — "I started writing
about it."

In regards to this poem, he says: "The poem is a reaction to A Course in
Miracles, which I have studied on and off over the years, putting it aside often,
but always coming back to it again, because its non-dualistic metaphysical
teachings regarding love, the world, the body, are so maddening, strangely
seductive, and beautiful, that while I can't quite swallow the Course whole,
I also can't stop dipping into its healing version of forgiveness. Like Helen
Schucman, the Course's 'scribe,' said about the Course: 'I know it's true.
I just don't believe it.'"

Now in remission, Hostovsky is a widely published poet and Pushcart
Prize winner. He is the author of four poetry collections: Bending the Notes
(2008), Dear Truth *(2009),* A Little in Love a Lot *(2011), and* Hurt Into
Beauty *(2012).*

He lives with his wife and two stepchildren in the Boston area, where
he has worked for the past thirty years as a sign language interpreter. He has a
daughter, twenty, who is a junior at Gallaudet University in Washington, D.C.,
and a son, twenty-two, who is also living and working in D.C.

MORNING MASTECTOMY

by Michelle Fimon

She's standing there, rubbing sleep from her eyes,
glistening tear not from sorrow but sun.
Waking only in body, she's refrained from
coming into the morning like most would do…

Instead, called… into a field of women,
lining up north and south of the interstate
wanting to dance and yet unable.
Their feet… and hers…
planted into generations of races:
the dirt and yellowing soybeans, Indian corn,
decaying leaves of stalks now stripped.
Skinless beings standing tall. Smooth stature,
outstretched arms; hundreds and hundreds
of white appendages, slicing the air onto her plate.

Like them, there's no end to the women
whom they represent — proud, faceless beings.
Mothers, daughters, sisters, grandmothers, aunts, nieces.
In the midst of the new mommas
is where she fights for life,
holding dreams that have begun to slip away; dawn cracking
an egg, sunny side up, into the day. Arms
that cradled babies, washed them tenderly, rocked
them to sleep… now clutch at air. Whirling windmills
slicing. Slicing. Slicing… Counting sheep, backwards…
ten nine, eight… slicing bread, warmed from the oven;
this is how the afternoon will feel. But for now,
fresh raspberry jam, cool cream.
Air still chilled.

Cutting the atmosphere. Cloudless.
Just the cold, sharp blades where her breasts
should be. Wind turbines, they're called by
those who created them. Instead she sees
her fellow sisters, lined up in rows across
the Midwest and the world, up at the breaking
of dawn, sharing the breaking of bread, the making
of bread… the making of love with a body
so foreign… mechanical — arms moving,
around and around… kneading the silicone loaves
into the fabric of her shirt,
pressed tightly to a chest where
nothing else remains.

———

Michelle Fimon had already endured unthinkable trauma prior to her breast cancer diagnosis in 2008: She'd been bullied in high school; was stalked and stabbed at eighteen; had been a victim of domestic violence; and was, at forty-three, raising a three-year-old son after a divorce. In the midst of cancer treatments, she learned her son was on the autism spectrum. That year, both mother and child experienced isolation and struggled with their identities.

Recognizing that a sense of belonging is a necessary component to emotional healing, Fimon found herself drawn to the wind turbines along the highway she traveled to Mayo Clinic for chemotherapy. Soon, she pictured strong, courageous women lining up proudly despite the presence of blades, which threatened their bodies.

Fimon not only wrote "Morning Mastectomy" to honor all breast cancer survivors, but she took part in a photo shoot in the very fields where the wind turbines are located. Early one morning, a photographer captured her dancing and twirling in the windmills' shadows, with arms and shirt open wide. The photos were paired with her poetry as an exhibit. Fimon's son, Jadon, went on to win a poetry contest in kindergarten and is featured as the youngest poet in The Cancer Poetry Project *("Gone," page 149). They make their home in southern Minnesota where cancer is not welcome.*

MOTORCYCLE

by Rebecca Pierre

She passes a motorcycle
gleaming black and chrome
by the side of the road,
a red For Sale sign
riding the handlebars.
She laughs aloud
at her sudden rush
of desire to own it,
to ride it,
to feel alive in the wind,
helmetless.
She imagines the bottles of pills popping
from her pockets;
the drip bags, needles, tubes
whirling around her,
finally flying free
as she roars through her life
like a tornado,
wild and reckless,
sucking up joy.

During her own chemotherapy treatment for lupus and kidney disease, Rebecca Pierre, sixty-five, shared the infusion room with cancer patients — "from young people to elderly people, male and female, all hooked up to needles or tubes."

"When I saw the motorcycle one day," she says, "I thought of us all — and especially the woman who laughingly pulled off her wig when I told her what beautiful hair she had. It made me think of how much we all would love to be free from these ties to treatment."

Pierre's poetry has been published in several literary publications and anthologies, including The Cancer Poetry Project, *volume one. She lives on an island off the coast of North Carolina. She is a freelance writer and a clay artist. She has two daughters, "who have given me a grandson and three granddaughters — including a set of twins — to love."*

OKAY

by Eric Weil

A few days after the biopsy, the nurse calls.
"You have a little bit of cancer," she says.
The C-word engenders the chill of mortality
while I stare silently at the kitchen counter,
phone stuck to my ear. I want to ask
if that's like being a little bit pregnant
and if I should schedule chemo, radiation,
surgery, organic enemas, acupuncture,
trips to Mexico, Thailand, and Switzerland,
and if I should stop saving for retirement,
give away my books, get my "things" in order.
I'm ready to fight and give up at the same time,
and I say, "Okay." "Now don't start getting
all crazy on me," she says. Crazy? Crazy
is accepting a death sentence with equanimity,
crazy is not regretting all the wasted hours
in a short life, crazy is not wondering how
I'm going to tell my wife and kids, or not
wondering how long I'll be able to work
and whether I paid that life-insurance bill
in the desk. So I say, "Okay." And she says,
"Come in tomorrow and the doctor will explain
how we're going to take care of this." This.
This unwelcome guest, the body's junk mail,
mutant cells growing in my skin
like a masked cabal plotting to usurp
my life. "Okay. I'll be there."

Eric A. Weil, fifty-nine, calls writing poetry a "way of life" and, thus, a natural response to his experience with squamous cell carcinoma.

Weil's poetry has appeared in The Hurricane Review, Wild Goose Poetry Review, The Greensboro Review, *and others. He has two chapbooks:* A Horse at the Hirshhorn *(2002) and* Returning from Mars *(2009). He also reviews books for Main Street Rag.*

Weil is an English professor at Elizabeth City State University in North Carolina. He is married with two adult children. By the time of publication, he expects to be a doting grandfather.

PEELING AN APPLE

by Janet S. Meury

Peeling an apple
Reminds me so vividly
of my grandpa Anderson,
sitting easy in his big chair,
slicing the red skin off in one long circular
snake, falling away from the pocket knife
in his broad hand. Year later, making pie, Mom
taught me to bring off all the peel in one piece like that and throw it over
my left shoulder to reveal
the initial of the man I would marry (always easy
to imagine the right letter). Grandpa had eyes the color
of Colorado high-country skies, almost too blue
to believe. And they twinkled, the way I always
imagined Santa's would. He wore OshKosh
overalls, and he handed out small pieces
of the white apple to us kids. It was
such a treat. Mom never peeled them just to eat.

Now here I am, sitting in my own big chair,
taking the skin off this lovely organic Honeycrisp
and popping pieces in my mouth, thinking this one
is living up to every inference of its name, so good
that I keep closing my eyes to savor it
on both sides of my tongue, wondering
whether Grandpa had stomach troubles too,
which made the peel hard to digest. He worked
forty years for the Union Pacific Railroad,
yardman and brakeman. He made homemade
root beer, which later transformed into Grandaddy's Secrets,
our family's name for root beer floats.

I know he laughed, told stores and jokes, but
my memories are silent tableaus: I watch him hitch up his
pant legs and dance around the room, everyone laughing, but
I hear nothing.
Later he died of throat cancer — too soon
for me, still in high school, to ever know him
better. Mine is in the lungs, under control now,
but whispering the dread that I too may end up
leaving grandchildren too soon. I must remember
to peel an apple for my girls.

———

Janet S. Meury, sixty-four, has been treated for breast cancer and continues chemotherapy for inoperable, incurable lung cancer.

"One of the blessings I've found from my cancer and chemo is the fatigue, even the 'bad' days, that confine me to the house and force me to accept sitting still for long periods of time. Stillness is food and drink to a poet!" says this woman, who has been "listening to, reading, loving, and trying to write poetry since I was seven years old."

Meury belongs to the West Thumb Poets, shares authorship of Listening to Stones *(Pronghorn Press, 2004) with poet Sheila Ruble, and has had her poetry published in anthologies and journals, including* The Florida Review *and* Boar's Tusk.

After twenty-seven years as branch librarian in Powell, Wyoming, she retired and now lives in East Helena, Montana, near her son, daughter-in-law and twin granddaughters.

PLANTING ACORNS, FAIRMOUNT PARK

by Lynn Hoffman

the pain came back, big, dull, personal.
it returned to the old neighborhood
and moved in next door to
where it used to live.

he recognized the pain, of course,
and of course, he had forgotten
all about it.

the tests showed what
the shows always test:
that the patient don't have long to wait
and that he could believe
but in the end, the end
was written with the beginning.

he gathered acorns from the sidewalk
and the road and the beds of his neighbors'
pickup trucks. he filled a bag with
a brown, promiscuous mix, two pounds, three.
dense, heavy, damp.
he sawed the straw-end off a broomstick
and went to the woods, poking and planting
each acorn on its side two inches down
gravely safe and covered in forest dirt.
he spread the empty bag on a spongy stump
and sat and looked along the way he'd come
and imagined first the dusting then the full sudsy
slather of the coming white concealing snow.

Diagnosed with oropharyngeal cancer, Lynn Hoffman, sixty-eight, was moved to write this poem after "waking up to the shaky nature of 'recovery.'" A widely published poet, he writes cancer poetry, "because it takes poetry to get to the heart of the matter."

In addition to approximately sixty-five published poems and a Pushcart Prize nomination, Hoffman has authored several books, among them, The Short Course in Beer, The Bachelor's Cat, *and* Paula Sherman and the National Rifle Association. *He is a food writer in Philadelphia.*

POSTED NOTICE FOR PILEATED WOODPECKER

by Laura L. Snyder

Every day between 10 and 2 p.m.
I will stretch myself on the trunk
of this pine tree until you come,
plant your spurred toes,
cock your ear, listen,
tap, tap, tap,
tap on me.
Turn your red-plumed head, listen,

and tap, tap, tap. I have chosen
you for your obsessive compulsion
to rid trees of their unseen invaders,
that rat-a-tat tat, rat-a-tat tat
that sounds clear through heavy fog.
Don't stop, woodpecker, find the cancer
with that kind jackhammer beak,
pound, chisel out
these cells dividing rampant.

Laura L. Snyder, sixty-one, writes poetry about cancer to "turn the unbearable into art." This poem, previously published in Classifieds: Anthology of Prose Poems *(Equinox Publishing), sings with quirky humor and a love of the natural world.*

In 2012, Snyder published two chapbooks: Winged *(Flutter Press) and* Witness *(Willet Press). Other recent works by Snyder can be found in* Baseball Bard, Switched-on Gutenberg, Fault Lines, *and* Windfall. *Her work is also included in three new anthologies:* Hot Summer Nights, From Glory to Glory, *and* Cradle Songs.

Snyder is retired, but now her work is writing poetry, canning, and gardening. She has "three children, five 'grands,' and a tuxedo cat named Baker, who brings me dead rats to inspect." She lives in Seattle "but would rather live in the wilds in a cabin and cook on an old wood stove."

REMEMBERING AND FORGETTING, 2011

by Dennis A. Norlin

Completing a medical history form for a new physician,
remembering doctors and nurses,
hospitals and procedures,
listing them in sequence,
talking with the new physician,
receiving a prescription,
paying the bill,
driving home,
suddenly remembering,
I forgot to write: colon cancer (1989).

———

Having survived so long — twenty-two years — since his first bout with cancer (colon), Dennis A. Norlin, seventy, forgot to include that information when completing a new medical history form. That experienced sparked this poem.

"The irony is that two weeks after writing the poem, a large, undetected sarcoma tumor ruptured, and I was roller-coastered into a five-month period of surgery, antibiotics, and chemo." Today, he is managing his cancer, which returned about seven months later, with more radiation and chemo.

While Norlin's articles on theology and religion have been published in scholarly publications, this is his first published poem. "I found that cancer produces all kinds of feelings, images, moods, and creative feelings," he says. "Maintaining a healthy, positive outlook calls upon all of one's creative and resiliency resources and skills."

Norlin is retired with three children and six grandchildren. He and his wife live in rural Beulah, Michigan, on a small lake.

RIGHT TO LIFE

by Patti Marshock

These are my hopscotching little ones who
grow exponentially, ten to the ninth.
They double and double again. I see them with
their arms spread wide, buoyant in warm streams,
building their homes along canyon walls and on mounds
of soft red clay. Some are sleeping and some dance in the dark,
dreaming of valleys, rich and fertile, that lie in wait for their arrival.
Intent on this process of finding new soil,
they don't listen to the carefully thought-out reasons,
why they should slow down… stay put.
In the shudder of cold wind, they are sheltered and cling
to one another, concentrating their efforts, and produce more,
better, stronger children. Stubborn in the cause, they carry themselves
to distant lands, following paths not made for their restless feet.
They love the places they find, they settle and make more babies,
feed them with the motherland's blood and sugar.
These are mine.
The scars on my left chest, just above my heart.

*Patti Marshock, a breast cancer survivor, is a nurse at the Mayo Clinic in
Phoenix, Arizona, specializing in work with cancer patients. She has published
poetry in* Disquieting Muses Review, 2River View, Fragments, Tryst, Ludlow
Press Poetry, Poetry Midwest, *and* The Cancer Poetry Project, *volume one.
She keeps busy with "work, friends, and my lovely family."*

SECOND CHANCES

by Tracy Rothschild Lynch

It isn't enough to be handed your life,
delicate as an encyclopedia page,
for you to protect.
You are expected to make something of it too.
Craft it, fold it, bend it,
shape it.
Shape it up.
You tell yourself that again
and again,
and yet again.
Sometimes it is part of what you pray.
A promise of sorts.
Or sometimes
it's all you've got to say
to God
or to anyone.
Because you do know
it's good to be here
with your life in your hands,
and there are ways —
there have got to be ways —
to mold it
to shape it
        up
and into something entirely new,
a life you've never seen before
and don't recognize.

Your breasts are gone.
The cancer is gone,
they say.
And you are
    here.
      Still.

Holding this life,
finally looking in the mirror.
In fact,
you look familiar.

---

*Following a bilateral mastectomy with 40 lymph nodes removed, plus chemo,
radiation, and ovary removal, Tracy Rothschild Lynch, forty-three, accepted her
"five-year prescription of Tamoxifen to ward off any more bad-guy cells forever
and ever, Amen."*

*A creative fiction writer and editor, Lynch says she has always written poetry
in secret. "A friend gave me* The Cancer Poetry Project *when I was in the thick
of chemo. I couldn't read it for quite a while — months, actually — because
when I picked it up, even the very first poem I opened to spoke such beautiful
truth to what I was going through and who I had become: a cancer patient, a
cancer survivor. Poetry is a beautiful 'secret code' for those who have been affected
by cancer — we can put together the words, form the memories of our own
experiences, and take another step in our healing process simply by knowing that
someone else gets it."*

*Lynch says she wrote this poem, in part, because of the pressure cancer
survivors put on themselves to learn something from their experiences, to (as she
writes in the poem) "make something of it." She explains, "It's often an unspoken
pressure, and I am learning to take a step back so I can stop, breathe, smell the
proverbial roses, and enjoy the life in front of me."*

*Lynch lives in Glen Allen, Virginia, with her family. Husband Mike "took
over all 'jobs' of a mommy during my illness with grace, humor, and tremendous
support. Daughters Kylie and Cameron, both middle schoolers, taught me the
most during my illness. Witnessing the experience through their eyes made me
stronger, more determined, more passionate. The depth of their love for me is
astounding and mutual."*

SIXTY-FIVE YEARS PAST LIBERATION

by Elizabeth Rosner

You learned early that life was
booby-trapped: land mines lurking
beneath the tablecloth,
so that at breakfast, usually,
someone exploded over
soured milk or a speck of
blood in the soft-boiled egg.
Bitter coffee was never quite
tamed by sugar, no matter how
many teaspoons-full you added;
caraway seeds from the
toasted rye would
stick between your teeth.

By mid-day, catastrophes
multiplied like stars.
There were dangers on sidewalks
as well as the highway;
strangers in the market
aimed dark sideways looks at you.
Trust no one, the instructions
promised. Don't you
read the newspaper?

Your mother in hiding
declined the name Survivor;
your father, beyond the Camp,
refused the same word
for his own reasons. So you
deny it too, now that you
understand something about
the body's surrender.

When the diagnosis came —
a phone call from the surgeon
on the morning of your
birthday saying, Why don't you
come into the office so we
can talk? — the kitchen
tilted and the chair lost
its solidity, yet you recognized
the arrival of the inevitable.

Maybe now, at last, the worst thing
was already here. You ate
your cold cereal and sipped
tea with something like ease,
a moment of utter, improbable calm.
Hadn't they warned you
it was possible to stay alive?

---

*Elizabeth Rosner, fifty-three, was diagnosed with breast cancer on her
forty-ninth birthday. Now in remission, she says she wrote this poem on the
first anniversary of the end of her treatment.*

    *"I was profoundly aware of the ways I felt (and still feel) uncomfortable
calling myself a cancer 'survivor,' preferring instead to say 'I had cancer,' or
'I went through treatment for cancer.'" She wrote an article for* Huffington Post
*on the subject, referring to the "s word" and its "complicated meaning in my life
as a daughter of two Holocaust survivors (who both had their own complicated
feelings about the word survivor). When I shaved my head during chemotherapy,
I was fascinated as well as disturbed to see how much my face seemed to resemble
the face of my father at the age of fifteen when he was a prisoner in Buchenwald
concentration camp. I had seen that photo of him, attached to his prisoner file
card, because he had managed to save it when the camp was liberated."*

    *Rosner, who writes "poetry about everything," has a multitude of poetry
credits; a chapbook called* Gravity; *essays in* The New York Times Magazine,
Elle *and several anthologies; plus two best-selling novels,* The Speed of Light
and Blue Nude. *Her forthcoming novel is* Electric City.

    *Rosner lives in Berkeley, California, where she is a writer, writing teacher, and
editor. She leads writing workshops and retreats throughout the United States.*

SLOAN KETTERING

by Lynn Mayson Shapiro

One thing they don't tell you about Sloan Kettering
is how beautiful the workers are, shepherdesses, sirens,
brawny football players, ready to lift the heaviest bodies. One,
rosy as a mountain child moves like the most even glare of light,
never turns away till you have risen to follow her.
She holds your paper file near her breasts, but not too tight.
Walls are paved with photographs, scenes of mountains, forests
carved by light. The chemotherapy suite is a skylight, a bubble.
You pass posters for support groups presented on easels like paintings
in progress. There are private rooms for each patient with chairs
and blankets and a straight backed chair for a companion if you have one,
and a little television with its snake arm, riveted into the wall.
In the center of all these private rooms are gatherings of high stalked flowers,
magenta, purple, amber, bursting higher than churches, in golden vases
everywhere, and the carpet is gold too, so padded you can hear
no sound of walking. There are so many workers here,
and your surgeon, Alexandra, is the most beautiful worker of all.
Her office where you wait is the color of cool green and mountain cream.
There is a computer pulsing out deep blue insignias. Next to it
is a magazine, half the cover missing, torn, or half eaten,
waiting for you to touch it in the same place as the person before you.
You don't and this decision, its stillness, its inability to reverse is profound
and stagnant. Outside, in the hallway other doctors stand leaning, writing
with the concentration of animals eating food, whose only purpose
is to become blind to everything but their own sustenance.
And she is the Sun. She is beautiful when she enters, says How
are you? You lean on her are. She opens your robe like the earth,
and you say, *I used to have beautiful breasts,* and she says, *You still
do,* and she cups your breasts. This is her special way. She cups
each one, then combs down, down with her fingers as if down
the side of a mountain she is scaling tenderly so as not to fall
once. She half closes your garment and you close the rest.
You watch her fingers leave your robe how they arc in the air

to papers on her desk, and you realize that at various times
in the past five years you have thought of her fingers, their short
nails, and how she called you and said into the mouth of her phone,
really as an afterthought, that *in the site of the malignancy we found
a little milk. A little* she said, like the purr of a cat, and you could see
her fingers, her surgeons fingers holding her own children's milk bottles,
and then as you will always, you will want to be like her, to save lives
during the day, then go home, feed your children at night.
You remember the way out on the soundless carpet.
Your husband is with you, murmurs, your husband,
the lobby, just as you remember, in subtle shades, tones green and gold.

---

*"My wife, Lynn Mayson Shapiro, was born in Washington D.C., and raised in
Cambridge, Massachusetts," says Erik Friedlander. She attended Smith College
and graduated from New York University. She choreographed for her own company, The Lynn Shapiro Dance Company, and won several awards for her work,
among them fellowships from the Guggenheim Foundation, The Jerome Foundation, and The New York Foundation for the Arts.*

*"Since 2001, Lynn had concentrated on her writing. 'Savage Love at Beth
Israel,' a piece excerpted from her memoir was published in the literary journal,*
Fifth Wednesday, *and was nominated by the board of editors for a Pushcart
Prize. She had works published in* Rattle *and* Mudfish. *This poem, 'Sloan
Kettering,' won the Pushcart Prize in 2008 and was inspired by Lynn's
experience at the cancer center during her initial treatment in 2001, and the
special relationship she had with her surgeon, Alexandra Heerdt. Lynn died
November 19, 2011, and I am very pleased that her thoughts and words
continue to move people — she would be very pleased."*

SWALLOWTAILS

by V. Jane Schneeloch

1.
Every summer I look for
these striped tigers
with their fearful yellow symmetry,
and multiple blue eyes
peering out from
frayed black fringe.

I plant
Asclepius and Buddleia
to lure them,
but it is the Monarch
who hovers above the nectarines.

2.
The doctor points
to small white flecks
on the dark film.
See? he says, some *abnormality.*
Another doctor says, *Cancer,*
and I must put that word in a sentence
beginning with my name.

3.
This summer the Swallowtails are everywhere.
They glide by as I park my car.
They fly through the yard to the tulip tree.
I see them on Sumner Avenue amid traffic,
at Quabbin next to the old stone walls.
How do I hold this abnormal abundance
in this fissure of my life?

V. Jane Schneeloch, sixty-seven, was astounded to see swallowtails — butterflies she had always loved — everywhere the summer of her breast cancer diagnosis. "It was a summer full of cancer and its worries," she says. "I didn't expect this, but then, who does? At the same time that I was forced to consider my own mortality, I kept seeing these butterflies everywhere — something else unexpected but very beautiful…. Poetry helps me see things I might not have seen otherwise — connections, contrasts, mysteries. Maybe writing a poem will help me find the answer to a problem, or maybe it will leave me with a mystery."

Schneeloch's chapbook, Climbing to the Moon, was published by Finishing Line Press in 2009. Her poetry has also appeared in literary magazines including Common Ground Review; Equinox; and Hello, Goodbye. Her play, In Hiding, was produced at the Drama Studio in 2008.

Schneeloch is a retired high-school English teacher, who works as office manager for the Drama Studio, a conservatory acting-training program in Springfield, Massachusetts. She has "four wonderful nephews" and a brother who lives nearby. Riley, her Lhasa Apso, is her "constant companion and was my comfort during my cancer treatment."

THIS, A BIRTH

by Anne Kelly-Edmunds

I catch my reflection
    in the mirror:
asymmetrical breasts.

My right always was
    a little larger
than my left,
    even before the tumor,
even before the cut,
    one-quarter gone now.

Placing right hand
    under right breast,
left supporting left,
    I mimic African sculpture
where a woman's hands
    under her breasts
symbolize generosity
    a peaceful welcome.

Anne Kelly-Edmunds, sixty-three, is a twenty-year survivor of breast cancer and may be facing "round three, as enlarged, hyper-metabolic lymph nodes were evident on recent PET scans. I feel fortunate and grateful for these many years of life, love, and shared good times since my original diagnosis. And, I look forward to many more!"

*   Kelly-Edmunds wrote this poem after she suddenly and unexpectedly saw her body in the mirror several months after breast surgery. "My poem is about coming to terms with the unwanted body changes wrought by the surgery for cancer. It is about the process of acceptance, even of the disease itself." Her first book of poems,* The Promise, *was published in 2012; she is working on a collection of memoir-based essays.*

*   Kelly-Edmunds offers creative-writing workshops on Long Island where she lives with husband Leland in Mount Sinai.*

THIS CAMP

by Lenore M. Montanaro

I march along white linoleum,
My fellow soldiers around me. We wear
Backward robes of faded paisley.

Each day we meet at the clinic's large main room
Where disbelief and reality collide —
Nothing can be this real.

I've painted my bald head with paint so red
It's like the blood each of us share,
United here, without hair.

We look at magazines of the newest styles:
Long hair and painted faces are in.
What's out? Who's who now?

We're child soldiers, not volunteers,
Draftees, into something like a war
None of us ever wanted.

Today the sores in my mouth
Mirror the growing sore in my body.
I could be a time bomb.

But please, no purple hearts today —
Just vibrant red ones. Only a soldier's heart
To survive this war, this camp.

When her nineteen-year-old brother, John, was dying in 2011 after six years of treatment for acute lymphoblastic leukemia — Leonore M. Montanaro, now twenty-two, sang "We Shall Overcome," changing the words to "You Will Soon Be Healed" as he passed.

Montanaro understood more fully than most people her brother's experience. At age five, she had been diagnosed with rhabdomyosarcoma in her right leg, and was treated with chemotherapy, surgery and radiation for eight years; in 2002, she lost her leg to cancer and now wears a prosthetic leg. She has been cancer free for ten years.

"'This Camp' is one of the first poems I've ever written," Montanaro says. "People often speak of fighting cancer as being a battle. Instead of viewing those who battle cancer as victims of disease, I view us as heroes.

"Many have told me that my suffering has led me to wisdom, but I have to disagree: Suffering has led me to learn empathy, which leads to wisdom.... Embracing my pain moved me to learn empathy so that I could feel the pain of others as well." She adds, "I'd trade my 'normal' life now for an 'abnormal' one again, just to have my brother back."

Montanaro's book, The Morning Within the Dark, *is a poetry collection funded by her alma mater, the College of the Holy Cross, Worcester, Massachusetts. All proceeds go to the John Montanaro Fund at the Ocean State Veterinary Hospital in East Greenwich, Rhode Island. During his lifetime, her brother had raised money for the hospital to enable people whose pets had cancer to afford oncological treatment. His efforts have saved dozens of pets from unnecessarily being put down.*

Raised in North Kingstown, Rhode Island, Montanaro is a law student at Western New England University School of Law in Springfield, Massachusetts. Her hobbies include playing the guitar, reading and writing, bird watching, and collecting all things "owl."

THIS TIME
— Lost Girl Island, August 4, 2008

by Lisa McKhann

I have this scar now up my middle, well…
it's somewhere between incision and scar,
fresh in the healing process, this time.
Hopefully, there will be more to come.
I look forward to a scar from hip-replacement at 70
or a fresh biopsy, like at 40, maybe my right breast this time,
say around 55? All the scars, I welcome.
This is my middle age, goddamn it.
I will live to 90 with all the beautiful
wear and tear of the aged.

Bring it on, bring on that weak-assed shit.
I am healing my body and this time,
it will come back stronger than ever.
I will swim to the island rock naked,
pull my sleek body, bald and hairless as a seal,
onto the granite slope, squat on the grey warmth,
northern August light reflected under my chin
like the dandelion game — Yes, I love butter! —
bathed in the mirrored perfection that is me.
When my skin grows warm and I am almost dry
I will wipe the last droplets off my arms and dive in
to swim, kick, stroke, reach, stretch, cut.
I will come gasping happy to shore.

By this time next week I'll be in
for Round Five — four down, two to go
but I will arrive stronger than ever,
so bring it on,
Let it scour my insides clean the way this lake
flushes my mind of all fear. Here I am granite.
I am water, a clear view down through 15, 20 feet
pristine with nothing to hide, pure sparkling good.
And on and on—I am cedar, white pine,
osprey and aspen grove and the plain sparrow's sweet song
so bring it on.

This time next year, and for many summers after
I'll be here again and still. Girl, woman, crone,
my body will always be strong for its age.
I will kayak calm mornings like this one, through the glint,
and write in new spiral-bound sketch pads, the thoughts
of an old, white-haired woman, with a long, thin scar
almost lost now in the softness of her aging naked hide.

Lisa McKhann, forty-nine, was diagnosed with ovarian cancer, stage 1B, four years ago on April Fool's Day. During the summer of her treatment, she offset chemo weeks with tent time, camping in the north woods. A writer and modern dancer, McKhann wrote "This Time" to "vent some of the ferocity that the body and spirit can muster, even when knocked flat."

McKhann lives in Duluth, Minnesota, with her husband, Peter Krieger. Since her diagnosis, she founded an online reflective writing site for cancer survivors and others, now part of the nonprofit, Project Lulu.

THREE MEASUREMENTS OF MY BREASTS

by Margaret Ann Towner

1. A WELCOMING
The first time
my sweetheart
touched me,
ran his fingertips
down my breasts,
I discovered
a universe of wants.
Through the opened
door, new possibilities
found me breathless,
face to face
with desire,
and Life
held out its arms
to welcome me.

2. PERFECT FIT
We used to find each other
in the stillness of the night
as you sought refuge
from the day.
My breasts were perfect —
you would tell me —
just the right size and shape
to fit into the palms
of your calloused hands.

3. BODY ART

In pre-op I sit on the edge of the gurney,
waiting for the surgeon, who arrives
with a black leather case of markers
in his hand. He zips it open,
shows me the variety of colors
and tips, proceeds to draw circles
and lines that crisscross my bare breasts,
chitchatting about this and that
as he makes his calculations.
No one has ever drawn on my breasts.
We want to make the correct incisions,
he says, as he admires his artistry.
And not to worry, later we can
tattoo nipples back on.

---

*After her diagnosis of breast cancer in 2010, Margaret Ann Towner's perception
of her body wholly changed.*

*"Losing my breasts was like an amputation," says Towner, sixty-one. "I even
experienced phantom breasts. When I was finally able to write, I wanted to show
my perception of my breasts before and after cancer, to capture those changes
through poetry."*

*Towner recently retired from teaching in Southern California. She lived for
many years in Latin America, has three bilingual children, translates poetry
from Spanish to English, writes children's music, and performs Latin American
music. She also has a poetry chapbook,* City by the Sea *(Pearl Editions, 2005).*

TUESDAYS

by Samantha Albert

Every Tuesday
the journey through Chinatown
to the chemo unit at the hospital.
The stench of garbage day, heightened in July,
threatens to overwhelm me
on those days when my stomach roils
with the effect of the drugs.
I pass front yards that are seeded with concrete
and porches of dilapidated student housing
that sprout old couches and beer bottles.
Tennis shoes drape from power lines,
the decorations provided by
drug dealers marking their territories like dogs.
I pass through all of this urban grit
with a mixture of fascination and revulsion.
Then I stumble upon them
and catch my breath with the deep green lushness
of the postage-stamp gardens.
Bok choi, tat soi, guy lan
peppers, eggplant and kohl rabi.
Vegetables that I can't identify,
but which make me feel I am in a foreign, tropical land.
These plants, growing so fervently from among the grit,
growing up, down, and out
to take advantage of every inch of space,
make me feel alive and supremely optimistic
as I leave Chinatown behind
and climb the four flights of stairs to my inevitable appointment.

Samantha Albert's weekly walk to the chemo unit through Toronto's Chinatown has a ritual quality, she says. "The neighborhood is vibrant, but dingy. There is something about these little, intense patches of garden that make me really happy, even when I'm not having a good day. I make a stop at each garden as part of my walk."

Albert, forty-five, was diagnosed with amyloidosis — a "close cousin to multiple myeloma," she says, in 2000. She underwent a stem cell transplant that year and, today, continues a weekly treatment with a new smart drug. "No cure, per se, but the disease is controlled."

Why write about cancer? "What better way to say the unsayable?" she asks. "How better than poetry to capture those feelings that are sliding around inside my head that can't seem to flow through normal conversation. Poetry opens doors for those thoughts to come tumbling out in a way that captures their essence."

Albert has a poem published in Survivor's Review; *her other publishing credits include essays in* The Globe and Mail *and* Edible Toronto. *She lives in Stratford, Ontario, Canada, with her husband, son, and two pet rats.*

WATER IS SURROUNDING GRACE
(borrowing a line from Denise Levertov's "The Avowal")

by Elizabeth Macfarlane Jones

The first time through breast cancer
I held the image of me whole and well,
fully recovered in a place I love —
past biopsies — surgeries — and weeks of radiation.

It's a clear blue day, Lake Superior's
water warm and still,
giant potholes visible in the

sandstone below the surface,
carved by the churning action of
stones and waves.

I am on a broad ledge
accessible only by water
or down a steep cliff with a thin rope.

Naked, I slip into the water
to feel the soft silkiness surround me
as I float on the warm surface,

then dive down
to the cooler waters
of kettle holes below.

This time, before surgery,
Muddy Pond in Damariscotta, Maine
held my body.
I let the water brush my breasts,
pucker them with the cold, stroke them
with the eddies my arms made.

My sister and I, alternate-side breathers
who swim at different paces,
swam together across the pond,
catching sight of each other now and again —
each glimpse a surprise,
a confirmation of sorts.

Since I've lost my breasts, I swim suited at the Y.
The water is a warm embrace,
stretching with me long and thin. Swimming
on my back, I notice a new relationship between
my changed profile and the water's touch.

I ride lower these days,
as if swimming in a trough instead of
rocking through the surface,
the way my body used to —
breasts skimming above, my torso below.

Now, the absence of my breasts lies
beneath the surface — caressed —
my nearly bald head cupped as well,
as I make my way from one end — to the other.

Elizabeth (Becky) Jones, fifty-nine, was part of a writing group for cancer
patients when a writing prompt — Denise Levertov's poem, "The Avowal" —
inspired her poem. "Before writing this poem, I had not seen how strong the
thread of water's presence in my life and in my body's healing from breast cancer
surgeries, radiation, and chemotherapy had been."

Leader of bereavement writing groups, Jones says, "I see over and over that
writing helps us get beyond the set narratives we tell ourselves and our loved
ones about our losses and about our relationship with cancer." Her previously
published credits include Patchwork *and* Peregrine.

Jones is married and lives in Northampton, Massachusetts, where she works
as a hospital chaplain. She also has a private counseling practice and serves on
the board of Cancer Connection, a community cancer-support agency.

WEDDING DRESS JOHNNY

by Maureen O'Brien

Did you see the fools dancing to their wedding song?
How he tenderly palmed her bare back
above her scalloped satin?
"Fools" is harsh. But what else to call who we were

over twenty years ago,
secretly believing "til death do us part" would never,
never come.
I was beautiful that day,

with snapshots to prove it.
A five-foot satin train
spilled behind me on the altar
as I repeated the words,
"in sickness and in health."
But I knew nothing about love,
nothing until

this winter when the surgeon told us
my tumor was malignant,
and you and I once again
clasped hands,
stared into each other's eyes, this time

eight stories up in the hospital.
Later, after my surgery,
we were alone like on our
wedding night.
You untied my strings and washed my naked back

With a wet-nap,
cooled me with damp circles
and then softly blew
to dry me off in stark fluorescent light.
You want true love?

You want true love?
It's in my broken strand
of freshwater pearls,
in the one-size-fits-all hospital johnny
I traded my wedding dress for.

Maureen O'Brien, fifty-two, was diagnosed with colon cancer in 2010, six weeks after her husband suffered two heart attacks. "I wrote this poem to explore how our illnesses forced us to face the fact of death — our own and one another's," she says. "Writing about cancer allows us to express our feelings and shape them so we can find greater acceptance of the truth. It is easier to hold the overwhelming emotions — fear, love, grief — when they are on paper, in our hands, not just lost and swirling within."

O'Brien is the author of the novel b-mother *(Houghton Mifflin Harcourt, 2006) and the poetry chapbook* The Other Cradling *(Finishing Line Press, 2011). She teaches writing to "amazing teenagers" at the Greater Hartford Academy of the Arts and lives in Connecticut.*

The Cancer Poetry Project 2

WHAT REMAINS

by Charles Entrekin

Our orange cat, Scout,
too old to hunt, sits in the sun,
watches birds at the feeder.
Brown towhees ignore her.

Some days I lose my words
and my vision blurs. I am
watching bright yellow tulips unfolding,
like a loose woman
with her arms outstretched,
petals limp with opening.

My hand, bumpy with skin cancers,
shakes from an unconscious tremor.
I can stop it when I try.

I want to speak how
I am disorganizing and
diminishing by degrees.
So many balls in the air
I can't catch or find, still spinning
in the lost, and the found
like the splash of a leaping fish
reverberates with what remains,
a sound that's wet as the dusk.

After an operation and eighteen weeks of chemotherapy to deal with aggressive B-cell lymphoma (which had transformed from indolent lymphocytic leukemia), Charles Entrekin was moved to write this poem. "The ravages of chemotherapy left me so pared down in both physical and mental capacity, I wanted to document the emotional state I found myself in, in what remained."

Entrekin, seventy-one, has been clear of cancer for four years. "Cancer is an emotional experience," he says. "One has to transition to an understanding that life is amazingly strong and yet terribly fragile. Poetry is the only language I can think of that can deal with such an amazing dichotomy."

Entrekin's most recent publications include a novel, Red Mountain Birmingham, Alabama, 1965 *(El Leon Literary Arts, 2008) and a poetry collection,* Listening: New & Selected Works *(Poetic Matrix Press, 2010). For twenty-four years, he was managing editor of* The Berkeley Poets Cooperative *and* The Berkeley Poets Workshop & Press. *He is founder and managing editor of Hip Pocket Press. He also founded the creative writing program at John F. Kennedy University, Orinda, California.*

Entrekin has been a founder and director of three successful Bay Area computer companies, and currently serves as a board director of INNOTAS. He lives in the San Francisco Bay Area with his wife, poet Gail Rudd Entrekin (whose poem, "Shaving Our Heads," is on page 108). They have five children.

WHEN ALL YOU CAN DO

by C.A. Emerich

When all you can do is
raise your head just enough
to see a patch of sky

outside your window, you
learn to love the sky. When
all you have strength to do

is sit and watch the birds,
you come to love birds. When
you are at last able

to do much more, you treasure
what you lost before, and
found again. To see in the

smallest, everyday sight the
glow of beauty is to glimpse
magnificence of creation.

When C.A. Emerich, sixty-two, was in chemotherapy and radiation due to bilateral breast cancer, "there were days I felt so sick and hurt so much that there was very little I could do. Still, I saw beauty everywhere in the smallest things, particularly when I looked outside: colors, birds, the way the light moved across the sky, the way the shadows fell. One of the greatest joys during those days was sitting by my living room window and watching the birds that came to my feeder."

Emerich has written poetry, essays, and stories most of her life. During her cancer experience, "poetry was the best way I could express the sadness, anger, terror, and hope brought about by profound illness." Her poetry has been published in Poetic Soul, Survivor's Review, and other literary magazines.

A retired elementary school teacher, Emerich now spends her time writing, walking, kayaking, performing with a choir, and listening to music. She lives in Cupertino, California.

POEMS BY SPOUSES, PARTNERS, AND LOVERS

AUBADE

by W.F. Lantry

My darling, sleep a little now, the night is over, no
strange visitors have haunted us, the dawn has broken clear
and I am well this summer day, though fevers burned all night,
I can't explain their origin. Now we have much to do:
just yesterday, at evening, the altar cabinet came,
although the walls are still undone, I'll have them fixed today.

Sleep well, my lovely *sorcière,* you need the rest, it's been
a winter filled with untold wind, an overrainy spring
and all through those your illness made you weary every dawn.
It's summer now, you're well again, the garden needs some care
but all the elements are strong: our lotus blossoms swell
and I delight to think of what you'll say when they're in bloom.

Now deeply sleep, *ma petite fauve,* consume me while you dream
or find me lounging by the shore in gentle reverie.
I give myself to you, and this small cottage now is yours.
We'll rearrange each room to your delight, or let it go
since I'm imagining the way the sunlight tumbles in
around your dappled changing form. My lithe gazelle, awake!

"My wife was diagnosed with breast cancer in the early winter, then went through surgery and radiation, which left her weak and led to a great amount of worry," says W.F. Lantry, fifty-five. "But by early summer, most of the crisis was past, and we were able to turn our attention to our future life." Her cancer has not returned for more than five years.

Lantry's publication credits encompass print and online journals in more than twenty countries on five continents, in venues as diverse as Cha: An Asian Literary Journal, Istanbul Literary Review, Voices Israel, *and* Poetry Salzburg Review, *as well as a chapbook,* The Language of Birds *(Finishing Line 2011), and a full-length collection,* The Structure of Desire *(Little Red Tree 2012).*

Lantry, a native of San Diego, received his Maîtrise from L'Université de Nice and holds a Ph.D. in Literature and Creative Writing from the University of Houston. Recent honors include the National Hackney Literary Award in Poetry, the Lindberg Foundation International Poetry for Peace Prize (in Israel), and, in 2012, the Old Red Kimono and Potomac Review poetry prizes. He currently works in Washington, D.C., and is a contributing editor of Umbrella Journal.

THE BLESSING OF CHILDREN, 2

by Julie Cadwallader-Staub

It was just two nights ago
when we told the kids:

No more treatments for Dad.
The doctors predict three to six months.

So tonight when I go into our daughter's bedroom
to kiss her good night
and she is still wide awake,
I sit down beside her
put my hand on her shoulder
and say,
"Is it anything you want to talk about?"

"Oh, Mom," she says.
"Tomorrow I have two whole class periods
with that boy who's been smiling at me.
Oh, Mom, I just can't wait for tomorrow to come."

Julie Staub grew up with five sisters, her parents, and a dog beside one of Minnesota's small lakes. Her favorite words to hear growing up were, "Now, you girls go outside and play."

Staub graduated with a religious studies degree from Earlham College in Richmond, Indiana, in 1979. There, she had the good fortune of rooming with Jane Cadwallader, who introduced Staub to her big brother, Warren. Julie and Warren Cadwallader-Staub were married for twenty-three years, until his death from multiple myeloma at the age of forty-nine.

Cadwallader-Staub earned a Master of Social Work degree at Rutgers University in 1984. She has served as executive director of the Maternity Care Coalition of Philadelphia, the Vermont Campaign to End Childhood Hunger, and the Child Care Fund of Vermont. She was vice-president for community grant-making at the Vermont Community Foundation before taking her current position, grants director for the Burlington School District. Her poems have been featured on Garrison Keillor's "The Writer's Almanac," published in journals, and included in anthologies. She was awarded a poetry grant from the Vermont Council on the Arts in 2001 and a scholarship from the Vermont Studio Center in 2011.

BLUE MOON

by Cathy Douglas

Sweetheart,
Your disease came in stages, death all at once.
From your point of view, our marriage rests in the past;
you believe yourself gone from our home,
while change follows me in heaves and jerks.
All you took with you was a suit,
the rest fell on me — heavy
as a death bed dragged to the curb,
miserable as twenty black trash bags
lined up against a wall
gently concealed by drifting snow.

Darling,
something of a man's arm still resides
in the handle of our hammer, parts
of a man's life litter our garage
camouflaged as hardware.
Sickness even now winds itself with cold sheets,
while doubt fastens itself to our children's eyes.
I'll find everything when the weather warms.
Now, in the ache of winter,
I'm throwing away your cancer food:
applesauce, sweets, pudding,
chicken a la king bought in a hopeful moment.
Today your favorite ice cream went into the bin,
a pint of Blue Moon from The Chocolate Shoppe.
I didn't open it, only lightly pressed the lid;
underneath, a crackle of ice filled the gap
between what you ate and what you didn't.

Dear One,
it's not that I don't believe in ghosts,
rather that I'm too thick-boned,
too mundane to live with one.
I love you.
But I'm begging you now,
take your ice cream and go.

"Cancer is a huge life-changer," says Cathy Douglas, fifty-five. "There's no way to ignore it, so we'd might as well write poetry about it."

That was her approach when a crushing depression followed her husband's death from pancreatic cancer in 2010. "Taking care of all the physical things he left behind was a huge emotional burden," she says, "one I hadn't even thought about while we were all focused on him during his last months."

Douglas has had poems published in Strong Verse, Verse Wisconsin, Vox Poetica, Every Day Poets, *and other journals.*

She lives in Madison, Wisconsin, with one of two grown sons; the other is stationed in Fort Hood, Texas. She works at a metaphysical shop.

BREAST CANCER POEM #2

by Bill McCarthy

It's not like removing a bullet in the Old West,
where the whiskey-soaked doc drops
the lead fragment — clank — into a silver tray
and says, "Got it.
You're gonna make it, young feller."

This seems more exorcism than extraction.
When it's over they wheel you through sliding
glass doors as somewhere a clock starts
its count back from five years.

We step into a future fragile as new lake ice,
black water sleeping beneath us
like a hungry Grendel.
We hold hands; take cautious steps
listen through our feet for the crack or creak
that might tell us the moment he wakes,
ready to draw us under.
But all is silent.

In time our stride smooths.
We no longer look down.
I notice how well our hands fit together
no fumbling as with a stranger.
Our grip loosens; the grasp is lighter.

When we pause, my index finger traces
yours out to where its curved shore meets
the cool lake smoothness of your fingernail
following it to the sharp edge
going over, flowing under until
your finger closes around mine
and we keep walking.

Bill McCarthy, sixty-four, wrote this poem a short time after Kate, his wife of forty-two years, had surgery for breast cancer in 2005. "It is an expression of both the powerlessness and connection you feel when someone you love is living with cancer," he explains. In 2012, the cancer reappeared and Kate is again undergoing treatment.

A collection of McCarthy's poetry, Past Sins, was published by Trilobite Press (University of North Texas) as the thirtieth-annual edition in its chapbook series, Contemporary Poets Reading.

McCarthy lives north of Stillwater, Minnesota, near the St. Croix River, and counts among his family members two grown children and one grandchild. He is currently launching the W2W Project, which assists leaders as they transition from the corporate workplace to the world.

BY BREATH

by Gary Boelhower

If you hold the hand of a dying man
it will change you. You will learn to count
each breath, sit in silence in your own soft skin

and let time take as long as it wants.
You will learn the sun's ritual, the round path
it walks each day, the discipline and the bright wonder.

The tick of the clock will not annoy you
and if there is a word or two, you will listen as if
your life depended on it. Not much else will matter,

the dishes, the laundry, the paint
peeling in the summer heat. Sitting at the side
of his bed even when he is sleeping will be enough.

You may not be able to say exactly what
has changed, but you will pronounce your name
as if it were hyphenated, wedded to river, orbit, earth.

You will watch trees bow down before the wind.
You will breathe one breath at a time as if your
life depended on it, your whole life depended on it.

Gary Boelhower, sixty-two, cared for his partner through his long fight with prostate cancer. The final weeks included many hours of simply holding his hand as they experienced the deep presence of love in the face of death.

Boelhower's second book of poetry, Marrow, Muscle, Flight *(Wildwood River, 2012), chronicles the "everyday infinite affections" of a gay man who loves his children, creates a home with and grieves the death of his partner, and finds again how "the fierce river in the heart begins to flow." It won the Midwest Book Award in poetry.*

Boelhower lives in Duluth, Minnesota, with his husband, Gary Anderson. He is Professor of Theology and Religious Studies and teaches courses in theological ethics and spirituality at The College of St. Scholastica.

COVERING UP FOR GOD

by Karin B. Miller

Out loud, I say to friends and family,
"I'm a bit mad at God this week."

Inside, I threaten.

"I won't cover up
for you anymore," I say.
"Everyone knows that
we've all been praying.
Through months of clinics,
chemotherapy, CAT scans,
surgeries, nausea, night sweats,
pills and tubes,
we've been praying.
Family, friends, neighbors,
work acquaintances,
the woman who shaved Thom's head,
my mom's carpenter, my sister's pastor,
my brother's bosses, my dad's staff,
Bible study groups, entire congregations,
even a group of little old nuns way up north
and their bus driver.

"So now,
if Thom needs another surgery,
whose fault is that?"

Two weeks later:
the surgery finds
the lump on the x-ray is
just scar tissue.
Chemotherapy —
and perhaps prayer —
have zapped the rest of the
cancerous mess.

I collapse in a heap of tears
on a pew in the hospital's chapel,
shaking, crying.
It is over,
it is over,
thank God.

———

Karin B. Miller, forty-eight, was inspired to create The Cancer Poetry Project *shortly after her husband's experience with cancer and the birth of their first child, Gabrielle. Her husband has now been cancer free for fifteen years, and Gabi just celebrated her fifteenth birthday.*

*Miller's career has included writing consumer and employee communications for major retailers; writing and editing for numerous regional and national magazines, including B*etter Homes and Gardens, Midwest Living, Minnesota Bride, *and* Mpls.St.Paul; *and writing* My Name Was No. 133909…and I Sang, *the memoir of a dear friend and Holocaust survivor. Today, while she writes occasional magazine features, her chief focus is marketing writing for various clients. She also enjoys having her poems published in various literary publications.*

Miller lives in Minneapolis with her husband and their three children: Gabi, Joey, and Mia. She is most grateful to family and friends for all of their support during the creation of both volumes of The Cancer Poetry Project.

DISTANCES

by Joyce Meyers

On this sodden New Jersey
afternoon, gnats stinging
my scalp, I walk miles
for money to cure cancer,
thankful to science,
chance, your courage,
that you came through.

You are fishing in Vermont.
I picture you on a boat
in the middle of a lake
I've never seen, or laughing
over dinner on the shore.
Last year you were too sick to go.

Night falls. As I walk the circuit
of illuminated bags marked
with names of survivors
and the dead mothers,
fathers, children, friends,

I imagine you gazing out
over the lake under stars
brighter than any
you have ever seen, unfurling
each moment as if
there is treasure inside.

"This poem grew out of participating in a fundraising walk a year after the recovery of my husband [from tonsil cancer] while he was on a fishing trip," says Joyce Meyers, seventy. "The walk was a powerful reminder of how lucky we were that he was one of the survivors and well enough to go fishing. It also reminded me of others I knew who were not so lucky."

Meyers' poems have appeared in The Comstock Review, Atlanta Review, *and* The Ledge, *among others. She has received multiple publication prizes in the Atlanta Review International Publication Prize, and was awarded second prize in The Ledge 2011 poetry competition. She has two chapbooks,* Wild Mushrooms *(Plan B Press, 2007) and* Shapes of Love *(Finishing Line Press, 2010).*

Meyers taught English at the high school and college levels, then practiced law in Philadelphia for nearly three decades, specializing in first amendment law. She and her husband live near Philadelphia and have two grown children and one grandson.

THE EVENING LIGHT

by Warren Slesinger

The horizon holds no lofty notion,
      no mansion in the moving clouds,
no gate that opens for her to float

      on her bosom through the air.
She does not live there and then
      in her naked skin, but here and now

when she steps out of the shower
      warm and wet, I kiss her slender neck,
and smell the perfume from the soap

      in the hollow of her collar bone;
the tiles gleam, the air swirls around her,
      and the mirror fogs with steam.

Wholly mortal is my wife
      who does not foresee an afterlife
and who is not indifferent to her own demise,

      and yet, she does not flinch
when I touch a bone instead of breast
      underneath the skin graft on her chest

as smooth and plain as parchment
      and larger than my hand
that could not protect her from the knife,

      but she is not embarrassed
by her nakedness, and presses against me
      her other breast while she leans

to wipe away the steam,
and when I turn, our eyes meet in the mirror
and I do not relish the reflection

in that instant
of misgiving in which she waits
and wants to go on living.

Others see a brightness in the sky
and find a higher purpose
in the evening light, but she does not.

Her eyes merely redden with regret
at the thought of time passing,
and yet, she seldom cries

as though she chose
the uncertainty of life
as opposed to the uncertainty of heaven.

"Because of her expression, the depth in her eyes, and will to survive, my wife is more beautiful to me as a 'survivor' than when she was the junior prom queen of the University of New Hampshire," says Warren Slesinger. "If ever character is evident in the poise and presence of a woman who went through a radical mastectomy and radiation treatment, Betty Ann Slesinger is the living proof of it."

Slesinger graduated from the Iowa Writer's Workshop with a Master of Fine Arts degree. He has taught English and worked at several university presses: Chicago, Oregon, Pennsylvania, and South Carolina.

Some of his poetry and definitions have been published in the American Poetry Review, The Antioch Review, The Beloit Poetry Journal, The Iowa Review, *and others. For two years, he has been at work on short stories, one of which has been published in* The Alaska Quarterly Review *and two in* Short Story America. *Currently, he teaches at the University of South Carolina Beaufort.*

IN THE ONCOLOGIST'S WAITING ROOM

by Dolores Hayden

A red nylon windbreaker
droops from a wooden coat rack.
I notice it in April. I notice it again in May.
As I worry about my husband,
I observe the red jacket that never moves.

I ask the receptionist — she shakes her head.
I ask a nurse — she shrugs. No one knows.
I view it as the chemo jacket, the death jacket,
the garment of some very ill man
moved into a hospital bed through the rear door.

The waiting room is always full. Hours pass.
On the table there are a few issues of *Time*
from 1995. It is 2007.
On the walls, garish seascapes
buckle in plastic wood frames.
The oncologist is a noted art collector.

The oncologist may believe hardship
prepares souls for purgatory —
this is a Catholic hospital,
next to his office is a chapel
with a very, very large crucifix.
In the hall, a cart offers free books —
Souls, Purgatory, and You,
Life After Death: The Evidence,
and *Hello from Heaven.*

In June we have an appointment,
but the oncologist is nowhere to be found.
The receptionist pages the radiologist.
He looks down at his shoes:
"Didn't he tell you? Your husband's scans are bad."

I hold no faith. I'm low on hope.
I walk into the chapel and light two candles,
one for my husband,
one for the owner of the red jacket.

———

Dolores Hayden's husband was first diagnosed with prostate cancer in 1989;
he passed away in 2007.

Hayden writes about American landscapes and teaches at Yale University.
Her books include The Power of Place: Urban Landscapes as Public History
and Building Suburbia. *Her poems have appeared in many journals and*
anthologies, including The Yale Review, Southwest Review, Slate, American
Scholar, *and* Best American Poetry. *She's published two collections —*
American Yard *(2004) and* Nymph, Dun, and Spinner *(2010) — and*
received awards from the Poetry Society of America and the New England
Poetry Club.

KITTY SMILED

by Gary Young

Kitty smiled, pressed my hand against the fleshy knot in her belly, and said, it's the child we always wanted, or as close as we'll ever get now. A malignancy, not a pregnancy, was swelling inside her. She'd caress it with her palms, and as the tumor grew, she mothered it; she brought it to term. One night she woke with a fever, and I carried her into the hospital. Her wasted arms and legs made her belly seem even larger than it was. A woman asked, are you in labor? And she said, no. Then the woman asked, but are you expecting? And she said, yes.

from Even So: New and Selected Poems, *White Pine Press, 2012.*

Gary Young was diagnosed with advanced melanoma when he wasn't quite thirty. "My sweetheart at the time, Kitty, cared for me while I underwent several surgeries and an experimental drug regimen," he says. "Six months into my treatment, we discovered that Kitty had advanced ovarian cancer. My poem records some of the irony of the sick taking care of the sick, and the very sad irony of a woman who was carrying a tumor being mistaken for a woman in labor."

Young, now sixty-one, is a poet and artist whose books include Days, Even So, Hands, *and three award-winning books:* The Dream of A Moral Life, Braver Deeds, *and* No Other Life. *He has received a Pushcart Prize, a fellowship from the National Endowment for the Humanities, two fellowships from the National Endowment for the Arts, and the Shelley Memorial Award from the Poetry Society of America. He edits the Greenhouse Review Press, and his print work is represented in many collections, including the Museum of Modern Art and the Getty Center for the Arts.*

He teaches at the University of California Santa Cruz, and lives with his wife and two boys in the Santa Cruz Mountains.

LATE MORNING/AFTER DIAGNOSIS

by Michael Rattee

My wife sleeps with the cancer growing inside her
while I sit not reading

The pages of the book in my lap
riffle beneath the ceiling fan like calm water

but I am in a rowboat with one oar
or two oars and no one to help row

or perhaps adrift with no oars at all
panicked by the rushing current

just yesterday we were happily afloat
humming our familiar tune

neither of us heard the roar of the falls

---

*"The day the oncologist told us my wife's diagnosis we drove home in near silence,"
says Michael Rattee, fifty-nine. "We had been totally unprepared for such news.
We had been happily married thirty-four years and fully expected to grow old
together." While she sought refuge in a nap, he tried to read but instead composed
this poem. His wife died of liver cancer, just four months after diagnosis.*

*Rattee's poems have appeared in numerous literary journals and anthologies.
His poetry collections include* Falling Off the Bicycle Forever *(Adastra Press),*
Greatest Hits *(Kattywompus Press),* Enough Said *(Adastra Press), and* Calling
Yourself Home *(Cleveland State University).*

*Rattee resides in Tucson, Arizona, where he works as a software engineer,
developing Internet applications for use in education.*

LEAN

by Vicki Wilke

Diagnosis. The images begin, piercing your spirits,
no words to name the fear, the depth, the numbness.
It wraps around you like a smothering heat you
can't escape. And then you breathe.

Sadness and mirth mingle together in waiting rooms,
the scenes warm your heart, and break it. A young
man in a wheelchair, quiet, blank, patch over one eye,
his pretty wife confirms the next appointment as she
stands behind his chair. They wait for a car to be pulled up.
It's one of those long, short moments. Still behind him,
she wraps her arms around his neck, leans onto him —
no words, just love.
I try not to look, and the magazine I am reading is blurry.
I read the same line over and over, I don't know what it said.
All I could see, and hear,
was the love.

A little boy, maybe ten, sports a tall, furry green-and-white
Christmas hat. It bounces joyfully as he walks down the hall ——
he knows where he is going, leads his family on the way, wiggling,
along with his hat, seizing the season of hope, not knowing
that he's not knowing, what will come. Bless him.
Save him.

My husband is immersed in the world now, of radiation,
infusions. A nurse angel tries to find the vein, his like to hide —
mine would, too. He settles down for the hours, and an announcement
comes — *This is Madelyn's last chemo!* Applause breaks out
and I feel the sting. I don't look at him at first, feel the tears
sloshing through the space between us. Why tears — we'll be there
in three and a half weeks, but it's still an aching, that we
have to cheer at all.
And we hope for Madelyn, and for ourselves.

All the waiting, so much waiting, long hallway walks, elevator rides, white coats everywhere, alliances with moment-by-moment strangers, in rooms with familiar walls. You wish them well, hope for them, wonder, but not too hard.

Cancer, we name it, permeates all the lives you love, and those who love you, like dominoes, tap tapping the shoulders of one, and then another. You lean, and thank God for them.

Ten years ago, Vicki Wilke's husband, was diagnosed and treated for squamous cell cancer. In 2012, he experienced a reoccurrence and surgery. Today, the couple is hopeful.

To write her poem, Wilke poured over her journals. "I felt so thankful that I had written some of this down," she says. "I had forgotten so many poignant moments, the moments that give cancer a challenging but beautiful face of hope."

Since retiring from teaching elementary students two years ago, Wilke has been a semifinalist in five poetry contests, which has meant publication in the Broad River Review *journal; a poem in a children's book,* An Angel is Born; *and pending publication in* Little Red Tree Poetry Anthology.

Wilke is the mother of two "beautiful and amazing" daughters and grandmother of two grandchildren. She lives with her husband in Clarkston, Michigan.

MY TV FAMILY

by Pamela Manché Pearce

Tim Gunn guided me like a contestant on *Project Runway.*
"Make it work!" he said. I did and mashed morphine into banana.
"Carry on!" he directed. I did. I called hospice.

I rode shotgun in ambulances,
like Katie Couric in Dafur.
If she can do it, I can too.

I would have called *Mad Money* if I'd had the time.
"Help me, Mr. Kramer. Help me, Jim!
I need to learn the lingo of finance.
What should I do, Jim?"
The market's crashing.
Our money and my man are dying. I can't stop it.
I can't stop it from happening to me.
To us.

Dr. Oz gave me answers about how a person dies.
The real, hard scientific facts.
About how a body works and how it stops working too.
"What does terminal really mean, Dr. Oz?"

Oprah showed me a strong woman. But her husband never died.
She has no husband.

But I did, and he left moment by moment.
One moment he was alive and there were two of us in the room,
the next moment: one person and one body. A body which he left behind
for me to have.

The sun sets as the moon rises.
My husband is dead and the TV
comes alive.

I am never alone now, never.

I watch television.
In the living room,
where the hospital bed was.
I sit in the big house
in the big chair
and watch the big TV.

At bedtime I take a Xanax and
go to *The Office*.
I am not old.
I am not alone.
I am not a widow.
I'm wearing pantyhose and a new cardigan.
I'm falling in love with my co-worker, Jim,
and I don't care how many times I have to answer
the phone, "Dunder Mifflin, this is Pam."

————

Pamela Manché Pearce's husband, Barre Little, died of brain cancer a year after diagnosis. "A bereavement counselor suggested I read or watch something funny before bed," says Pearce, sixty-five. "'The Office' had the perfect time slot, and I had a place to go and people to see and the possibility of a laugh. Knowing I could count on this nightly event was a great comfort.... When the television was on, there was the sound of the human voice in my house, someone to eat meals with and times to look forward to."

She also found herself beginning to write poetry after many years of writing fiction, nonfiction, reviews, and performance pieces. Her writings have been published in numerous publications, including The Brooklyn Review, Mondo-Greco, *and* Playbill Korea. *She has performed her pieces at The Katonah Museum, The Cornelia Street Café and the Depot Theatre. She has two books in the works.*

Today, she is a hospice volunteer; a student at The Art Students League; and a founder of Poets Read Poetry, a quartet of Hudson Valley poets who discuss poems and appear regularly on radio, at public events, and as guest speakers. She lives in Garrison, New York, with her flame-point Himalayan cat, Snow-on-Fire, a.k.a. Snoofie.

The Cancer Poetry Project 2

NO BORROWED TIME
for Fred

by Carol Tufts

In the 1930s film, death is no more
than a plot device, a punctilious gentleman
tied into the flowering branches of an apple tree
by an old man whose time has come. A neat trick
were it not for the grainy black and white
of the moral. So much suffering outside
the frame until the old man's grandson is stricken.
The knotted ropes undone, Death slips back
into the picture as old man and boy walk together
through a telescoping porthole into the luminous
fadeout as I have walked into the absolute whiteness
of this small room with you, trimming my bookish armor
to invoke all of creation exposed for what it is
and is not as in the chapter on Ahab's whale.

Still, even Melville allows for provisional moments
of strange sweetness, the fragrance of ambergris
that does not slide itself over the naked space we breathe in,
its unrelieved scent of disinfectant and residue
of odds reeled off as if a bookie had taken bets —
eighteen to twenty-four months, future wagers closed.
Then here comes death, no genial gentleman of the perished
last century, but dressed up in your own flesh
with no stratagem to lure him into the springtime
extravagance of a backyard apple tree, the conceit
of all those blossoms that cannot fall.

Carol Tufts' partner, Fred, was diagnosed with prostate cancer in 2010. They have hope that "yet another hormonal therapy" will slow his aggressive cancer until the FDA approves the drug they are awaiting.

"I was moved to write this poem after an appointment with the oncologist," says Tufts, sixty-five. *He didn't seem knowledgeable about the latest treatments for prostate cancer, she says, and displayed a less-than-empathetic bedside manner.* "When Fred [also a physician] asked the oncologist for a prognosis, he said, 'Well, you will come back for another appointment in August. If the psa has gone up and there are more metastases to the bone, maybe eighteen to twenty-four months.' After this, he smiled and told a story about one of his patients who went on a cruise to Alaska, became obstructed and was unable to pee.... I felt as if I had fallen down the rabbit hole.*

"People do not like to talk about cancer, or the fact that something is going to take each of us from this world, that death is not an option, but an inevitability. Too many patients and those who love them too often feel isolated and helpless. Cancer has too often been at the center of my life, and so I am writing about what I know."

Tufts' poems have been included in various publications, including Poetry, Poet Lore, *and* The Journal of the American Medical Association. *She teaches in the English department of Oberlin College and lives in Oberlin, Ohio.*

THE PERMANENCE

by Yumiko Tsumura

It was into August,
your birth month,
when your oncologist told you
"you have come to
the end of your life,
so every morning when you wake up
do the most important first,"
and the doctor gave us a group hug
before parting.

That day
after coming home numb,
we laid ourselves down flat on the floor
side by side holding each other's hand
in the brilliant light of August,
with a cool green wind from the garden on our faces
listening to the silence
in the pulse of time.

Our eyes went to Miro's *The Pygmies Under the Blue Moon,*
the two pygmies playing with some preoccupation,
the blue moon in motion,
together we tasted
the kernel and
melted.

Outside the picture window
a hummingbird came to
the tiny red flowers
of salvia we grew
in our garden.

"I could not allow myself to fall apart and cry in front of my husband," says Yumiko Tsumura, sixty-three, "because he was the one in fatal helplessness and was not in a position to console me. Writing this poem gave me temporary solace from my own helplessness at that time."

Tsumura's husband, Samuel Grolmes, was diagnosed with prostate cancer in 1999, then esophageal cancer in 2003. He passed away in 2004.

Tsumura's book of poems, The Green Scream, *was published in 1968; her poems have appeared in major Japanese and American literary journals, such as* Kyoto Journal, Poetry Kanto, *and* Manoa. *Her books of translations include* Tamura Ryuichi Poems 1946–1998 *(CCC Books),* Let Those Who Appear *by Kazuko Shiraishi *(New Directions), and others.*

Tsumura was born and educated in Japan, trained in traditional brush writing (shodo), *and earned a Master of Fine Arts degree in Poetry and Translation from the University of Iowa. She taught American literature at Baika Woman's College in Osaka, and Japanese language and culture at Foothill College as a longtime resident of Palo Alto, California.*

SANCTUARY

by Meredith Davies Hadaway

In March, we drive again through the wildlife
sanctuary, bypassing the groomed ponds, dammed
and seeded to bring ducks and migratory geese.

We travel the back lanes, wooded and secluded, closed
to those who do not know these acres: a tangled
swamp of beaver huts, upended trees and twisted

roots, where turtles slip from logs as we approach.
Here we look for evidence. The osprey have returned
to splintered nests on platforms tilting

over water. They flap from pole to piling, ferrying
their catch headfirst into the wind and chirping a ridiculous
whistle, too small for such large birds. They are here —

back early — you point out as we stop the car to watch
a muskrat glide and disappear beneath its own ripple. One
more spring, I do not say. We turn the car around

and bump our way along the edge, turning the wheel
between pits and spreading puddles to avoid
the mud that swallows tires.

---

*"After my husband died, I felt completely adrift," says Meredith Davies
Hadaway, fifty-nine. "I did not set out to write about cancer, but, until I
confronted my experiences as a caretaker and a widow, found I was unable to
write about anything else."*

*Her husband, Cawood Hadaway, a wildlife artist and avid outdoorsman,
was diagnosed with stage-four lung cancer in 1999, "fought a courageous battle,
but passed away fourteen months later."*

Hadaway has two poetry collections: Fishing Secrets of the Dead *(2005),
which includes "Sanctuary," and* The River is a Reason *(2011), both issued by
Word Press. She lives on Chester River, along Maryland's Eastern Shore.*

SHAVING OUR HEADS

by Gail Rudd Entrekin

I say I'll shave my head, become a moon-
face-bald-pink-shining defenseless-
seeming creature in some kind of funny hat,

when your hair falls out in tufts on the pillowcase
in the morning, your crisp silver beard thins,
soft flesh under chin shows through.

When we shave our hair, our skin-covered skulls,
which we have never seen, will be revealed,
embarrassed in their naked whiteness,

their lumps and bumps and funny spots, no help
for the unfortunate contours of our faces,
our strange prominent noses or ears,

heads that haven't been seen by anyone
since we were babies and our mothers
ran their fingers through our delicate fuzz,

our fathers palmed our noggins
in their callused hands, admired how like
heavy fruit we felt, and wondered who was waiting
inside these perfect structures,
these elegant bony domes.

"*If you've never shaved your head, I recommend it,*" *says Gail Rudd Entrekin, sixty-four, who shaved hers in solidarity and support of her husband.* "*People look at you differently. It's interesting to be perceived in a whole new way, and it's fascinating and freeing to see your simple face, uncluttered by the distractions of hair.*"

Her husband, Charles (whose poem, "*What Remains,*" *is on page 73), was diagnosed with incurable (but remissible) chronic lymphocytic leukemia in February 2007.* "*Most days we remember to be mindful and to savor every moment of our lives,*" *she says.*

"*Shaving Our Heads*" *appears in Entrekin's newest book of poems,* Rearrangement of the Invisible *(Poetic Matrix Press, 2012). She and her husband are poets, editors, and former teachers of creative writing and English literature. They are also publishers of Hip Pocket Press, and she is the editor of the online environmental literary magazine,* Canary. *All of their five grown children live nearby in the East Bay of San Francisco.*

SILENCE

by Claire Thornburgh

I understand, now, why we hide
like sick cats
seeking a soft dark corner.
Faces freezing
others huddle, laughter distorting,
eyes chilled or skittering —
no kindly excuse
no bending my perception.

They do not ask:
How progress your disasters?
Have you coped this week
or month or year... ?
Stretching silence.
They turn instead
to anyone beside them,
or a passing car, or a cloud.

We have learned to find joy
where we overlooked it.
So they laud us, if they dare think,
as heroes or martyrs.
But it is only galling necessity,
like gratitude for another morning,
or the heavy plod of footfall
to the next task.

They are not as frightened.
Leave that for another day.
They likely wish me gone,
no more than do I,
resentment creeping
for their freedom to live
with dreams, complacency,
tidy rows of being.

---

*"My husband was diagnosed with stage-four colon cancer at the age of
forty-three," says Claire Thornburgh. He died two years later after typical
cancer treatments.*

*"I have always loved to write," says Thornburgh, fifty-one, "but it felt as
though I wrote to survive after my husband became ill. Sometimes I was inspired
by the love he and I shared, other times the horror of our battle, and in this
instance the feeling of being isolated, even ostracized, as we endured a situation
that did not make a pleasant basis for social interaction.*

*Thornburgh says she has been lucky enough to stay home with her children,
Faye, eighteen, and Charles, twelve. Both have poems in* The Cancer Poetry
Project *("Apparitions," page 130, and "Go Away," page 147, respectively).
She also enjoys sewing, gardening, and cooking.*

*Thornburgh and her family live in Seattle and have a lovely view over the
Puget Sound and the Olympic Mountains. "These days the fourth in our family
is my partner, Jeanette, who has helped to get us all back on track after the chaos
of illness and loss."*

STILL LIFE WITH PUNCH LINE

by J. O'Nym

There are only six hours left
in this day you dreamed: your wake
at which mourners mumble and marvel
at your spectacular lack of luck at losing
your life thirteen months to the day,
post cancer diagnosis.
Less than six hours remain, and you,
quite alive in the next room, are
strumming your Hummingbird, so
I needn't remark on the wood luckily
appearing here, at the end, or waste time
knock knock knocking.

J. O'Nym, fifty-three, is a bassist and a songwriter. Meg Hentges, a musician and "my everything for the past twenty-eight years," was diagnosed with breast cancer in 2010. Following a mastectomy, chemotherapy, and an oophorectomy, she is slowly recovering from damage done by chemo; there is no recurrence at the two-year mark.

"Now that cancer has completely flipped our world upside down, we are utterly changed," says O'Nym. "We want honesty and clarity in all things. Poetry is the perfect vehicle, like a clown car. Deep. And then deeper. Something worthwhile and new with each reading. Compressed language, powerful in its ability to move us, sustain us, heal us, challenge our assumptions. All excess cut away. Perfect art for us in this new existence."

O'Nym played in Hentges' band for years, and they write songs together, some of which can be found on her CDs: Tattoo Urge, Afterlaugh *(T/K Records), and* Brompton's Cocktail *(Robbins/BMG). Lately, they have been creating songs, photos, and drawings about her cancer. O'Nym's poetry has appeared in many journals and anthologies, including* Calyx, Borderlands, Runes, *and* Dirt *(The New Yinzer Press). They live in Santa Rosa, California.*

TOGETHER IN THE ICE STORM

by Henry Hughes

I'd pour burning vodka over the trees
if it would help
melt that killing weight. The thought works
for a while, until sadness extinguishes
anger's blue flames
and your hair drops long
into the white basin.
I'm sorry, I say, touching your back.
But you can't hear below those creamy falls,
roots slipping from tunnels of autumn's love
before the right breast sunk, before the chemo
and the Pacific sky
surprising with combination trouble —
a little harmless snow, then freezing rain, then cold cold.
Even the evolved go down like dinosaurs
in an ice storm.

Smoking a cigarette on the porch,
I hear the gunshot crack of a limb
that might save a groaning maple.
If only we'd make it to the sun —
crystal pains letting go
and shattering to earth
like windows of a cruel church.
Back inside for another drink, I see clippers
and a towel, your bald crown in firelight.
You're beautiful, I say, so close to truth,
it catches and burns.

"After my lover was diagnosed with and treated for breast cancer, we struggled with sex and love and how we felt about our lives and bodies," says Henry Hughes, forty-seven. "The poem comes from the day Lisa and I experienced a serious winter ice storm — it was the same day she decided to cut off all her remaining hair. There was something very violent, frightening, but, ultimately, beautiful and enduring about that experience. Poetry is the only way I could talk about it."

Hughes is the author three collections of poetry: Men Holding Eggs, Moist Meridian, *and* Shutter Lines. *He teaches writing and literature at Western Oregon University.*

VALLEYS AND LILIES

by Nancy M. Fitzgerald

Say our spouses died the
same day and
left us numb and needy
among children.

The lilies of the valley
by my back door never
bloomed that spring.

Say I met you
hollow eyes, but
ruddy in your red jacket
saw you steaming
in the snow shoveling out
my driveway.

Say you said, "I'll teach
your son to drive"
and I knew love at forty
felt different than at twenty-three.

Say my body aching from
his cancer and chemo
felt better curled next to yours.

Say I laid my head on your
chest and wept
for him —
Your cheeks wept upon my breast
for her —
Say we were healing partners.

Say all this is true
and that we survived
and from the valleys of our grief
grow lilies sweet and strong.

Nancy Madison Fitzgerald, seventy, a retired creative writing professor, was forty-two when her husband, Jack, died of bladder cancer. She met Jerry, her husband of twenty-seven years, shortly after their spouses died and they became "healing partners." She wrote this poem during that healing time. They did their best to finish raising their six children and now live in Northport, Michigan, in the summer and Tucson, Arizona, in the winter. "Reading, teaching and writing poetry has been my life," says Fitzgerald. "Over and over again, reading poetry has awakened me, and writing poetry has helped me find my way." Her new book of poetry, Take a Twig, *was published in January 2013.*

THE VISCOSITY OF HONEY

by Lori Tucker-Sullivan

I have spent the wrong season hibernating
and I'm not yet able to wake
and move.
Though the warm days are growing shorter
and overripe vegetables sag from the plants
in our neglected garden.

I walk in something the viscosity of honey.
Its ability to pull me down into a deep sleep is as sweet.

I will not look at the calendar until September,
and indeed the day planners
on our laundry room wall — usually overflowing
with activities, appointments, special dates —
blare at me with white emptiness.
I will think about life, and take part in its continuity,
when This is Over.
When I am not making daily treks to a hospital,
or striking whispered bargains into thin air.
I will live again when I can look without crying
at an elderly couple holding hands.

I make a deal with this disease, offering up a summer,
one short season: a few months
we should have spent vacationing.
Have it, I say. Take it.
I will spend these sunny days in waiting rooms,
sitting in infusion centers, reading in the ER,
napping with shades drawn to invoke winter twilight.

I cannot seem to speak the words "New Year"
for fear of sounding too self-assured against this threat.
And I fear the retribution crossing that line might bring.
I rub his bald head, try to joke about his lost memory.
I shudder as I feel his thinning frame beside me in bed.
I buy him hats, and together
we watch baseball games on television.
All in an effort to stave off, or give into.
As weeks turn to a month, I'm no longer certain.

In return though, I demand:
I want this disease out of my house (for good this time),
by the days when October's chill is on my skin.
Only then can I plan for birthdays and holidays,
what we might do for Thanksgiving,
or what will grow in next year's garden.

I want us to awaken. To see rain turn to snow
and know that this has passed. Though I also know
that there will never again be certainty.
A cough will bring fear at its most abject.
A headache will bring tears that paralyze as they fall.
I know that not all will return as quickly
as hair on his head,
or feeling to his fingertips.

Lori Tucker-Sullivan's husband, Kevin, was diagnosed in 2008 with head and neck squamous cell carcinoma. Writing poetry helped, she says: "It was a release of a lot of anger over why this had been visited on our family. My husband was healthy and took great pains to be healthy. He was a marathon runner, ate the right foods, and didn't smoke. And yet." He passed away in 2010.

Tucker-Sullivan, forty-nine, has had essays published in The Sun, Now & Then: The Magazine of Appalachian Studies, *and in local and publishing trade publications. She works for a group of independent bookstores. Her son, Austin, twenty, is pursuing a career in dance; her daughter, Madeleine, fifteen, is a high-school student. They live in Dexter, Michigan, in a one-hundred-year-old farmhouse that she and Kevin renovated.*

UNTITLED

by Douglas Dow

In the morning we sail from the harbor, the hotel marina.
This yawl, *Jada,* has such big sails, so amplified
when the wind erupts them.
I have your ashes in this metal box,
where you kept your tea.
Jada moves over the calm waters.
We pass fast-paced pleasure boats and
fishermen on the shore.
And we leave behind the mighty carrier,
the *Ronald Reagan,* whose barriers are
strung out, impenetrable.
In the warm sun, not much to fear,
but Kathryn says, "What if we sink?"
The captain reassures your daughter's child.
"The Jada has not sunk in all its years."
Our sails are filled. This useful friend, the wind,
brings us past Cabrillo Point, named long ago.
I think he was the agent of a former majesty.
I confess to Dana that yesterday,
at the bottom of our magazines, I'd come across
your last *New York Times* crossword — April, half done.
And today, in the side pocket of the car,
I found your Skin So Soft.
We arrive outside the harbor, in the ocean,
where it's deep and nearer Mexico.
Together, we wash you in amid the subtle
ocean swells; unhurried, you disappear.
Now I dream no discontent; the politics of life elude me now, no
shipwreck's creak.
The tide that took you, I do not fear.
Always with me, you say within a shell held to my ear,
"I'm ready for anything."

Douglas Dow, seventy-one, lost Rosalie, his wife of twenty-four years, to endometrial cancer in 2010. She had written with author Sharon Bray's Writing Through Cancer workshops, and she wrote "until the very, very end." Upon her death, Dow, a cancer survivor, "wrote this poem...to express my feelings about our loss. I wanted to say what one woman meant to us and just what it is that we have now."

Dow, now retired, pursued several careers, including driving a cab in New York City and serving as a job coach to developmentally disabled adults in San Diego. Today, he spends time with his extended family, reads, draws, paints, and writes. This is his first published poem.

WHAT I SAVED

by Karen D'Amato

It was the holes that got me
quarter-sized fruit of your scuffy slide
on an average day of pacing.
At the paper, I'm sure it drove everyone crazy
how you'd cradle the phone
and scrape back and forth, firing questions.

Home, I thought you kept moving
because your mother's icy stare
pierced every window. You couldn't throw away
that photo the three of you next to the Christmas tree
you bearded, nineteen, your father
boyish as ever — both with your arms around her
pretending she had the will and fight
to purge her lungs of poison
while she kept right on smoking.

Now I think your restlessness
was a deal — you carry her ghost-bones piggy back and
she closes her angry eyes and laughs.
You're gone ten years,
same as your mother when I met you.
So who has trouble letting go and who haunts whom,
you're so alive to me?

When we first knew your cancer was back
and I dragged you to a party to dance,
didn't we grow audaciously giddy?
We could whirl our way out of anything,
flirt, grind, tongue, sting, until you said
you had to sit down.
You put your feet up, out of breath,
I grinned and pointed at the holes
single burns mid-sole through layers of crepe,
and said, *He'd walk a mile for a Camel.*

Luckily you didn't smoke.
The nods from everyone in earshot
cheered us on the way home, but in bed
you were too tired, already one testicle short.
I fell back on the pillow and bristled
Domestic life is a washout —
words I'd never strung together
saved despite myself,

the way I saved one of each shoe
in a Blossom Hill wine box
so I could keep one of the battered pair
you danced in. By now
I've made some peace with this,
though I still add *tonight, only
tonight,* each time I play that minute back
wishing I'd rubbed your furry nape
and offered to wash your feet.

----

*Karen D'Amato, teaches writing at Curry College, where she also serves as
faculty advisor and editor of the student literary arts journal. Her work has
appeared in online journals,* Del Sol Review *and* Perihelion, *and in anthologies,
including* When a Lifemate Dies: Stories of Love, Loss, and Healing;
Summer Home Review I and II; *and* Eden Waters Press Home Anthology.
She lives in Jamaica Plain, Massachusetts.

WHITEOUT

by Melinda Driscoll

Silence.
Snow falls on our day
filling hollows, muting hard edges of curbs and steps
taking from our view intricate branches
and the green roof of our birdfeeder.

Unlike rain that you hear and smell
you only discover a snowfall
when you look up from your book or work.
Cancer in your body began that way.

While we prepare for tests, reports, more tests,
and try to picture your life emerging
from the promise of chemo-radiation
to kill aggressive adeno-carcenoma
and surgery that will eliminate one organ
and reshape another,
cancer cells feed and multiply.

We look at each other;
anxiety pins our stomachs.
There is no time for fear
or thoughts of life without you.

Dense heavy flakes sink to the ground
as you drive away in a whiteout
your face framed in the fogged driver's window.
Silence against silence, you recede.

The tumor has not metastasized.
Your profile is good, and
the doctors want you in their program.
Yet, we dare not hope beyond today's test.
Grim excitement lurks in our hearts.

Melinda Driscoll, sixty-two, lost her husband to esophageal cancer just a year after diagnosis. "He was a beautiful man and poet, and there is not better way that I can honor his life" than writing poetry about his cancer, she says.

Driscoll's previously published credits include Poet's Touchstone *(New Hampshire Poetry Society),* Sunflowers & Seashells *(second-place winner),* A Poet's Guide to New Hampshire 2010, Northwoods Journal, Granite State Journal, *and others.*

Driscoll works in marketing and business development for a family owned construction company. Originally from San Diego, she has lived in New Hampshire for nearly twenty years. She has one daughter who teaches, also in New Hampshire. She loves writing, art, cooking, photography, gardening, piano, and tennis. And she is learning to cross-country ski.

1-800-4-CANCER

by Alan Walowitz

My wife loves to talk about her work, but I don't love to listen.
Who wants the tales she has to tell?
With her pay come the horrors she's gathered that day:
Folks call the Cancer Hot Line and trade their woes for facts
though the facts are always sad.
One woman called to find out what *malignant* was.
What her doctor wouldn't tell her, the Hot Line would.

I don't think I could.
I don't even like to hear the word,
though I like to say words are my work.
She says, *It's crazy, these poems you keep making.*
I know she's right, but the making's what I like:
the click I make when I close the door behind me;
the music I make when I'm pounding these keys.

But, then, right in the middle, the telephone rings.
It's my wife wanting nothing again:
She says: *I just have to talk to someone well and sane.*
She says: *It's an epidemic and it's closing in.*
She says: *Cancer. It can make you fucking crazy.*

I'm no doctor. There's not a single cure in my head.
But I notice lately if I wait enough,
the ringing will stop.
I'm an ostrich, I know, and sometimes I'm crazy.
But even she finds me easy
when left to the healing
of my own tentative making.

Alan Walowitz, sixty-three, has been writing poetry for over forty years. This poem comes from the 1980s. "I didn't understand much about cancer — or poetry — then and I understand a little more now," he says. "Still, the emotion behind it — wanting to run away from cancer and hide from it — is still quite real and true, as far as I'm concerned."

Walowitz lives in Great Neck, New York.

POEMS BY FAMILY MEMBERS

AFTER THE DIAGNOSIS

by Annette Opalczynski

After the diagnosis,
dirty dishes pile up in the sink,
but the dog still needs her walk.
She pokes me with her cold, wet nose:
Remember me?
Outside she runs,
pulling me forward,
her ears flapping in the breeze.
My neighbor waves.
He's mowing the lawn
in his bare feet.
At the corner,
we pause to watch the kids playing
their daily basketball game.
Along the fence,
wild honeysuckle blooms
and I breathe in
persistent summer perfume.

Annette Opalczynski, forty-six, was feeling depressed after her father was diagnosed with lung and bone cancer. "But the dog didn't care; she still wanted her daily walk. For me, it was a metaphor for the way life goes on and demands your attention, no matter how badly you feel." Her father died a year later in 2003.

    Opalczynski's poems have been published in The Sun, The North American Review, Oberon magazine, *and* The Paterson Literary Review. *She was the 2009 winner of Farmingdale State College's Paumanok Poetry Award.*

    Opalczynski lives in New Castle, Delaware. She has worked nearly twenty years for the Delaware Department of Health and Social Services.

APPARITIONS

by Faye Madeleine Thornburgh

One of those Mondays where the air is heavy,
and holding you in, a cold, sweat-soaked corset.
The atmosphere spits up fumes that smell like
concentrated oregano extract.
This whole city feels unclean, needs a rainy baptism,
needs to be sun bleached.

I am sitting in the back of the car where,
still, the smog that swirls in the stomach has pervaded.
I watch the gloom and breathe through an asthma attack.
From the other end of a congested intersection
two shapes solidify among the pale, ill blue.
Under the red light beacon, the father taps the crossing button
with his brown-sleeved elbow.
His bald head floats over his brown sweater,
through the fog. His thin body looks like a jack-in-the-box.

The image softens.
There is a girl, maybe ten, holding his arm.
She has ribbons in her hair, and is talking to him,
mostly with her free hand, which enchants the air around her,
She conjures angels and sunrises,
as, finally, the light turns green.

The father smiles down at her, and we pass.
Herbal air steals them from view, but I keep watching,
until the little, red hand down the road becomes a white, walking man.
I knew those two people on one of those Mondays,
where the air is heavy and holding you close.

Faye Madeleine Thornburgh, eighteen, learned the meaning of "cancer" with her father's diagnosis in 2006. He died of stage-four colon cancer "on the grayest Valentine's Day imaginable" three years later. After dabbling with poetry in middle school, she found her voice after her father's death. Themes of cancer, fatherhood, and loss weave into much of her writing. One of her poems placed third in a 2012 Seattle Times *contest. She also has contributed her voice to several poetry slams and community readings. Apart from poetry, she reads, knits, and runs role-playing games for her friends. She attends Seattle University and misses her family, which includes two more poets in* The Cancer Poetry Project: *mother Claire Thornburgh ("Silence," page 110) and brother Charles Alden Thornburgh ("Go Away," page 147).*

BAKED BEANS: A WORD FROM THE DEAD

by Mara Faulkner

How I long for a voice to break
the long silence,
a country strange and vast without sustenance.
A word in dream or vision to say, "I'm safe home. I'm happy.
    I'm myself and more, the person you knew and loved
    and didn't know."
Day and night I'm listening
    but not a word
    my brother as silent in death
as he was in life
    when his mother and sisters waited months or years
    for a letter or a call
    as he trudged West, shedding possessions and people.
Just at the end he turned and flashed a smile,
    and then was gone.
Though he's in that new place where distance disappears
in the twinkling of an eye, or so they say,
he is as silent as God
    withholding comfort
    in the conspiracy of death.

But then from the friendly darkness of my recipe box
    I hear his voice, laughing, defiant — sandwiched between beets
    and broccoli bake
    his instructions for baked beans, sent just before he died:
    "I use pinto beans but I suppose great northern would work too. I just
    don't trust anything that is white. (Does that make me racist?)
    Mix in two tablespoons of mustard (make this stone ground not that
    yellow crap that people put on hot dogs).
    Bake at 250 for 9 hours."

These are earthy words.
   Like dreams and visions they tell me only what I know:
   In a kitchen smelling of onions and molasses
      feed each other food cooked slowly while you laugh and talk
      and do good work.

It isn't much.

People have lived on less.

Mara Faulkner, OSB, seventy-two, wrote this poem after her brother's death. "Dennie's illness changed his life and him," she says. "Instead of thinking that he could go it alone, he turned to family and friends, spending time with his children and grandchildren, his sisters, brothers-in-law, nieces and nephews. Some of us got to know him again after years of distance. I was one of the lucky ones."

   Faulkner, a cancer survivor, has several publishing credits, including Going Blind: A Memoir; *"Things I Didn't Know I Loved," winner of the Foley Prize for Poetry awarded by* America Magazine; *two additional books, several poems and essays.*

   Faulkner is a member of St. Benedict's Monastery in St. Joseph, Minnesota. She has taught literature and writing for almost forty years at the College of St. Benedict. She plans to retire in 2013.

BARN WISH

by Kim Knedler Hewett

You are in the old barn
Getting so dirty Mom won't let you in the house,
Then kicking mud off your boots against the back step.

Not on a couch in our dark living room.
Covered with wrinkled blankets I've never seen before.
Not being moved by three nurses
With serious faces
To the sitting room that now has a hospital bed
Beside the sealed-up fireplace
And a piano that needs tuning.

I sit where you can't see me
Listening to the rustle of papers and pills in the other room,
Wondering if you can hear them.

Let's go back to the barn, I whisper.
Let's turn on the TV and watch the Bengals lose.
Let's eat Bill's Doughnuts and drink Pepsi.
Anything but this.

Kim Knedler Hewett, forty, wrote this poem about her father, Ircel Knedler Jr.,
on the first anniversary of his death. He was first diagnosed with esophageal
cancer in 2008. After treatment, when a second round of tumors showed up in
his liver and kidneys, "our family was devastated. Dad had always seemed in-
vincible, even through the entire fight against cancer. I never thought it would
beat him.

"My father was a strong man—a six-foot tall, tanned farmer. He worked
in the Ohio fields his entire life, raising cattle, hogs, and crops to support our
family. He was a quiet man, my own John Wayne, and he had a beautiful
singing voice. He died in the same farmhouse where he was born, seventy-five
years later."

Hewett works as a copywriter and marketing manager for a high-tech
research-and-development firm in Dayton, Ohio. She lives with husband
Michael, two sons, one very hyper dog, and a bad cat.

THE BATH

by Connie Levesque

Shoulders pale beneath a russet mane,
she might have posed, once, for a painting —
Woman at Her Bath — by Renoir, perhaps, or Rossetti.
And I, her sister, now hand-maiden,
come to sluice warm water
down the plain of her back,
to coax her thick wet hair into frothy foam
and rinse, gently, mindful of the dressing
on her breast. Beneath the gauze, a wound
I cannot cleanse, I can only bend to the task
at hand, as women have done across the ages,
witness to each other's naked hopes.
And as she rises, Venus on a half shell,
I sense the eyes of the artist hard upon us,
his hand poised above the canvas,
our two lives trembling at the tip of his brush.

---

*Connie Levesque's sister was diagnosed with triple-negative breast cancer in 2009
and is in remission. Says Levesque, "I wrote the poem for my own catharsis and
to honor an especially vulnerable but tender moment between us." Levesque has
a Master of Fine Arts degree in creative writing and lives in Portland, Oregon.*

BLAH, BLAH, BLAH

by Ellen Collins

Blah blah cancer
Blah blah stage 4
… sorry
Sorry
We're so sorry
I'm so sorry

Blah blah Jesus
Blah blah prayers
Flowers! Balloons! Get well soons!
Thanks. Thank you. Thanks. It's lovely. They're lovely.

Call
Card
Visit
Call
Card
Visit
Flowers. Plants. Books.

Blah blah pain
Any pain?
Blah blah love you
I love you
We love you
love you love you love you
love love love love love…

Ellen Sarafan Collins, fifty-three, wrote this poem shortly after her beloved sister-in-law was diagnosed with stage-four glioblastoma. "I have lost many — too many — friends and family members to cancer and stand with close loved ones who are currently battling this scourge.... I have buried my father and the children of dear friends. My sister carries the Lynch syndrome genetic mutation, and my sister-in-law has brain cancer. In my family, we don't worry about cholesterol. Instead, we wait. Sooner or later (please, God, later), it becomes our turn. My relationship to cancer? I guess you could say I am the witness. And I am waiting." Collins is a lawyer who lives in Florida.

CAREGIVER BURNOUT

by Marissa Cohen

moment to moment, you flash in and out like a bad neon sign:
Mom, gone, Mom, gone.

I never knew I could be this strong.
it never occurs to me that
no one should be this strong.
you were not meant to sit, eating McDonald's
(because that is what someone gave us)
in the psych ward because cancer is taking your brain,
and so we're here with the homeless and the crazies,
waiting for a room in the main ward,
because no one in the world knows
what else to do with us.

you're supposed to be home, with dad, except he died last year.
I'm supposed to be anywhere else, maybe in love, maybe traveling the globe.
I'm twenty-six and you are only fifty-six. it doesn't matter.
we're never old enough for this.

a tweaked-out homeless guy throws a recliner across the ward
and when it hits the nurse's station, glass and pandemonium explode like your
bad cells. a patient knocks on the door of our room because he has to pee
and thinks this is a bathroom. I tell him to go down the hall.
behind the door, my fist closes into a hard shell.
dude, don't come in here. don't! I'll drop you.
i'm used to thinking on my feet, now.
he slinks off. it could have been a close call, he could have
forced his way in, gotten rough. everyone on the ward was busy
picking up glass. a night nurse tackled the chair-thrower.
you never know what can happen. there's only me to
protect you. (what else is new?)
I'm destroyed, but I'm ready.

later, the nurses make me cut the belt off your favorite robe.
it's routine. it's our normal day, mommy.
I take the offered scissors, slice off the belt.
you are down the hall (only sometimes sure who I am),
writing with crayons because I can't bring pens.
last year, you were top in sales.
you remembered everything about me, including my name.
now, I have no name, there is nothing left to know.

Marissa Cohen, thirty-four, wrote "Caregiver Burnout" to describe the years spent taking care of her terminally ill mother, Deborah, who succumbed to lung cancer and brain mets in 2007. "The experience described in 'Caregiver Burnout' is a moment of supreme isolation and determination amid bleak circumstances," Cohen says. "As a nontraditional-aged caregiver in my twenties, I had to learn how to survive in a drastically altered universe. I ultimately learned that transformation and love are the only ways through hardship — it's a lesson my mother would have applauded. If writing about cancer shows one caregiver that she is not alone, I've succeeded in my mission."

Cohen's writing can be seen in She Magazine, TheDesoto.com, Gather Kindling, *CBS Radio, Chemistry.com, and in many other print and web publications. Cohen edits* artifacts, *the newsletter for the Stonewall National Museum and Archives. When she's not writing, Florida-based Cohen spends time with friends, family, and Mugsy, a bouncy rat terrier.*

DEADLINES

by Kelly Nelson

Dawn. Haul my body out
for a thirty-minute run.

For breakfast, the usual: blueberries
on cottage cheese with ground flaxseeds.

I've screened myself for everything, consulted doctors
about removing the removable parts. I swallow B vitamins

with wheatgrass juice, forgo beer and mojitos,
never touch cold cuts, check the batteries in the fire

detector, avoid freeway driving,
take yoga and meditate, and now this news:

Whitney Houston found dead in a tub
at forty-eight. My age. The age my dad was

cut down by cancer.
I decide no more baths, only showers,

superstitious to this inherited deadline. I've 121 days to live
as long as he did, 122 to live one day more.

Kelly Nelson's father died at age forty-eight, two years after being diagnosed with prostate cancer. "I was in junior high school at the time and have been spooked about getting cancer myself ever since," says Nelson, forty-nine.

"When I turned forty-eight," Nelson says. "I figured out the date when I would be the exact age my father was when he died. I'm not sure I would necessarily recommend doing this; it became a powerful preoccupation. ' Deadlines' was written during the weeks leading up to this date." Nelson's poetry has appeared recently in Paddlefish, Dash, Ozone Park, *and* Eclectica.

She lives in Tempe, Arizona, where she teaches Interdisciplinary Studies at Arizona State University. She also serves on the Tempe Municipal Arts Commission and volunteers as a gallery docent at the Tempe Center for the Arts.

DRAFTING YOUR WILL

by Anna Di Martino

Sitting at the table
pen and legal pad in hand,
we're figuring your life
in fractions.

One lifetime
divided by two children
and two grandchildren.
It seems simple enough,
but the math is more complex.
What exactly is
one quarter of your home,
and who decides
which quarter they should have?

Is it the quarter with the kitchen,
meat-sauce simmering on the stove
and you at the sink,
cursing the vinyl window
with the too-wide frame?
Or the quarter with your bedroom,
and your bed, all too familiar
with your frail form?
Please leave that to someone else.

This is the quarter I want:
I want a quarter of a lifetime of your laughter, and all
those crow's feet around your eyes.
I want a quarter
of my freezer stocked with chicken broth
you knew I wouldn't have time to make.
I want a quarter of your body
wrapped around mine
when I'm in bed with chills,
too sick to feed my kids.
I want a quarter
of a million Sunday dinners
with you and your stories.
I want a quarter
of the garden
planted by your hands
for a quarter of eternity.

Anna Di Martino and her mother met with an attorney to draft her mom's will. "It was a difficult experience for both of us," says Di Martino, forty-three. "It made me consider all the things I really wanted from my mom, none of which were concrete, material things."

Her mother, diagnosed with stage-four colon cancer, was told she would live, at most, twelve months; she lived for over four years, passing away in 2012.

Di Martino is the director of a small, nonprofit preschool in San Diego, where her mother volunteered twice a week the last year of her life. "The children loved her," she says. Di Martino's family, including two daughters, lives in Mission Hills, California.

FIVE MUTATIONS

"In order for a cancer to develop, there has to be five separate mutations.
I've figured out each of mine."
— My twenty-one-year-old sister explaining her thyroid cancer to me, fourteen

by Aviva Kasowski

Hashimotos: another disease, characterized by a thyroid
the size of a brazil nut. It seized her gently between lattes
swallowed in preparation for big, pre-medical exams.
She always scored ahead of the curve;
thus, the disease was non-limiting, almost innocuous.

Radon: a gas. Unpinnable, intractable, seeping upstairs
from the 1800s underground railroad in our basement
where runaways watched their breath in candlelight. It rises,
then falls through the lion-footed porcelain bath spout
like violet light shrapnel. The sinister glitter
in the outer horns of vision, after standing up suddenly.
In dreams, it takes the form of horse manure
that I fall into, becoming paralyzed, shrinking my lifespan
to the spike of its half-life raised to the second power.

Genetics: Father's side of the family: Texas farmers,
"backwards" Poles. A bright cotton field: the birthplace of self-feeding ambition.
Flat-chested aunts with hairy legs (and glands the size of ostrich eggs).
My father first saw a vagina at age five when his 26-year-old sister
lifted up her long skirt to take a piss.
Mother's side: Jews. Schetel dwellers turned New York City
egg sellers. The Bronx before it went Black. A closed community
where smoky basement furnaces harkened unspoken memories.
My grandmother took baths as the handyman fixed the plumbing,
for nakedness was the least of all evils.

Randomness: Shit happens. Mutant cells refusing
to commit suicide.
But if God exists, why does He allow good people to suffer?
If the "good person" is you, then the answer is simple:
God doesn't exist.

"The Animal Paper" (Stress): A fifth-grade assignment
I only heard about, how Mom made her stay up all night,
researching the eating habits of jungle animals
so she could win the first-place prize
of a Merriam Webster's Dictionary, and go on believing
as long as you worked hard to be the best,
your life would be a beautiful story.

*Aviva Kasowski, twenty-eight, grew up on a large horse farm in Pennsylvania,
and has since lived in Los Angeles, Israel, and New York. She holds a Master of
Fine Arts degree from the University of California, Riverside, where she received
a Chancellor's Fellowship of Distinction. Her work has appeared most recently in*
Spillway Magazine, The Packinghouse Review, *and* Zocalo Public Square.
*She was a work-study scholar at the Bread Loaf Writers' Conference in 2012.
She teaches test-preparation and enrichment classes at public schools in Queens
and the Bronx.*

The Cancer Poetry Project 2

GO AWAY

by Charles Alden Thornburgh

Sirens are blaring
"Are you awake?"
My sister looks scared.
Paramedics run up the staircase.
Mom and Grandma rush up, too,
followed by more paramedics with a gurney.

"Oh, no. Dad!"

I run upstairs after everyone.
CPR.
"His lungs are not working."

I don't ask, "Will he die?"
I already know.

Needles, machines, voices.
Mom holds Dad's hand,
cries.

He sees me and says one thing,
through the oxygen mask:
"Go away."

He didn't mean it that way.
But I'll never forget that it was
the last thing my dad said to me
on the day he died.

"It helps to write about things that are hard," says Charles Alden Thornburgh, thirteen. After three years of illness and treatments, Thornburgh's father died of colon cancer. "I was prompted at school to write of an incident that was important in my life. I knew this story would be compelling." This is his first published poem.

Thornburgh is not the only poet in the family. His mother, Claire, and his sister, Faye, have poems ("Silence," page 110, and "Apparitions," page 130, respectively) in The Cancer Poetry Project 2.

Thornburgh, a seventh-grader, likes school, his Seattle neighborhood, and his friends. While soccer and basketball are his favorite sports, he also likes computer games.

GONE

by Jadon Fimon

Today I got a sticky grabber from Perkins.
It cost one quarter and came out of the machine in a plastic egg.
    It looks like a little lizard.

My green chameleon is so great; he can fly in my imagination.
    With a long tail I can stick him to anything I want.

I swing it around like a helicopter blade.
I once watched Mayo One blast off into the sky
    'til I couldn't see it anymore.

I sling my sticky grabber onto my mom.
    Maybe it will take her cancer away…

Jadon Fimon, now seven, was only three when his mother, Michelle, was diagnosed with breast cancer. It was an especially difficult period for both of them that year: While Michelle was losing her breasts and hair, Jadon was being tested for autism. Although the school district labeled him with both Asperger's and ADHD, the tests also revealed that he's academically gifted. Jadon now receives his education via an online public-school format at home, allowing him to focus his talents and thrive, especially in the creative arts.

In kindergarten, Jadon won the Richard Eberhart Poetry Contest for "The Stormy Night," and he gave his first public poetry reading at age five, when he also wrote "Gone." (His mother's poem, "Morning Mastectomy," appears on page 40.) Jadon, his mom, and the sticky grabber make their home in southern Minnesota, where they all celebrate the fact that Mommy's cancer is gone.

GREYHOUND BUS

by Sherry Dee-An Coffey

What better vessel to transport me
from solitude to family, writer to daughter,
retreat to treatment.

Look at the young girl perched on the front seat,
carried from mom to dad, from south
to north, from one system to another.

What better courier than this? A racing
hound, retired perhaps, but loyal, always loyal.

Slick black nose coming to rest
on my knee, looking for attention.
My hand caresses his silky ears.
Ah. Blessed canine comportment,
taking me away from where
thoughts rest and are not uttered
to places of verbal failure:
how are you?
How strong to carry all of us on your back.

Grey is the color of February sky, of clouds hanging low,
not this or that, but in between — my mother living,
now dying. Praise this bus,
how else would I keep arriving
to say good-bye?

Sherry Dee-An Coffey, forty-two, was inspired to write this poem on a bus after a two-week writing retreat, heading to the Cross Cancer Institute to visit her mom, Margaret Rose Coffey, who had been diagnosed with stage-four uterine or cervical cancer — "it had progressed so far they couldn't be sure. Coffey says she was "thinking how circumstances in life change quickly and how a bus is a great metaphor for that in-between space — from what was, to what will be. I was also thinking about loyalty and companionship and how dogs portray those traits so well."

Coffey's previously published credits include poetry in Room Magazine *and* The Northern Review. *She was one of ten recipients of the Lieutenant Governor of Alberta Emerging Artist's Award for her novel manuscript,* A Pattern of Walking, *in 2008. An excerpt of that manuscript was also awarded the Writers Federation of New Brunswick's Richards Prize for fiction in 2006.*

Coffey is married, with a young son and a fat cat. The family lives in Fredericton, New Brunswick, Canada, where Coffey works as an after-school child-care provider in her home. "This work allows me up to five hours of creative time for myself in the mornings, and also allows me to be with my son after school." She is an advocate of community gardens, urban agriculture, and fresh, local food.

HOSPICE

by Philip Cate Huckins

When my mother got the call from hospice, she declined the offer.
"If you can get here by this afternoon,
we can provide you with a room." She told them that she
could not find a place for her cat that fast. So, well, thank you, but no.

"Bring your cat," the woman said. So we packed
a few bags and Barney and set off for Concord.

We had known hospice was in our future
as soon as Dr. Hampton had said that the chemo
Mom was being administered was not helping,
that even with that regimen of what was essentially
engine coolant being poured into her body,
the CA-125 numbers were not coming down,
in fact, they were rising, and this was Mom's third round.
So he signed the papers saying that she had
the right number of months to live to be eligible for admission.

When we arrived, we were given a tour. It was a lovely place, really.
Kitchen, dining room, TV room, overnight accommodations for visitors,
if the need ever arose, and a room for family and friends
to gather that offered some privacy.
And the room in which she would be staying.
It was a bright room. Windows on two sides, chairs,
bathroom, a closet, and, in my Mom's case, a box of kitty litter.

Each morning my mother was greeted by a staff member or
a volunteer who would ask how my mother was doing and what
they might provide in order to make her more at ease.

"So, Sarah, for lunch, a baked potato,
slathered in butter, with bacon, topped with M&Ms?"
No. Not today.

It took Mom a while to get into the rhythm
of hospice, but once she did, she went all in, in her own way.
"Sarah, how can we make your day better?"
Being a Yankee, she demurely offered, "I miss my birds."

One of the staff members heard what my mother,
the Yankee, was saying. The next morning
there was a beautiful feeder filled with thistle on one side,
black-oil sunflower seed on the other, and she awakened
to an explosion of avian color and sound. That was Tuesday.

On Thursday a volunteer asked my mother
the magic question, "Sarah, how can we make your day better?"
With the nearly deafening success of the previous request
still ringing in her ears, she tried her luck again. "I miss my flowers."

The next morning she woke to a vibrant, variegated garden
that had simply arisen, much like color had suddenly appeared
to Dorothy as she made her way to Oz.

With the feeder and the garden, the staff had made my mother
so much more alive than she would have been
looking out the window at the parking lot.

On a Friday, a few weeks later, while my brothers and I
stood by her bed, we knew it would not be long.
At about ten in the morning her last breath left her.
The birds were singing. The flowers were blooming.

Philip Cate Huckins, fifty-three, and his brothers were amazed at the compassionate care their mother enjoyed during her experience with ovarian cancer from "the most thoughtful and loving and compassionate people on earth, none more so than the hospice staff members" in Concord, New Hampshire.

"The beauty of the ministry of hospice is that it is not a place to die," he says, "but rather a place to truly live one's last days to the fullest, to be present and whole until death comes.... If a poem can reflect that [care], then perhaps it will act as a palliative, reducing some of the trepidation related to the unknown, for both the person who has cancer and for their loved ones." This is his first published poem.

Huckins is a professor of education at a small college in New England. He lives in New Hampshire.

I CAN TAKE IT

by Micah Chatterton

We had a trick for pain.
He would clench one or two of my fingers
when we saw the hot moment coming, whenever
we had the luxury of preparing ourselves,
and as the bandage ripped, as the tube pulled
or the needle dug, he'd crush my fingers
as hard as his small hand could grind.
He'd bend them sideways, rolling
my knuckles like stones in a backflow.
We imagined the pain passing from its source
like gleaming dye, up through the estuaries
of his body, through his stronger arm
and back into the rock of my fist.
He truly wanted to hurt me, not to punish
me for letting the doctors claw at him,
but to keep from being alone
in the dry white spotlight of suffering.
I always lied a little, exaggerated
his strength, wincing and sweating, setting
my jaw to let him believe he could break me,
to show him he was not alone, to show him
how to let these things happen
and go on.

On the last day, his tumor damming
the nerves from brain to diaphragm,
his body was forgetting how to breathe.
He could not speak, except for hand signals —
a weak thumbs-up, a flipped bird, "eat," "sleep," "milk."
As his chest began to still like sailcloth,
I held a Good Humor bar to his lips, read
Psalms and Dogen. I made up a story
of two heroes who were caught in a storm
and blown to opposite shores of a black ocean.

They never stopped loving each other, always
carrying pictures of the lost one in their minds,
always searching. After many years, they found
each other again on some warm, unmapped
coast, so they knew then they would always
find each other. I tried to prepare him, to comfort
him by being strong enough to let this happen.
I didn't want him to fear for me too.
"Imagine the pain coming from your heart,
up through your shoulder, down through
your arm, into your hand, and then my hand,
because they're the same," I told him, gasping.
"Give me your pain, Ezra."
He clasped my fingers as hard as he could.
"I can take it," I lied.

———————

*Micah Chatterton's ten-year-old son, Ezra, was diagnosed with stage-three
thallamic astrocytoma in April 2007.*

   *"His doctors expected him to only have three months before the cancer over-
took his brain," says Chatterton, thirty-two. "He lived eighteen months, until
October 2008, through chemo and proton radiation, through many losses and
setbacks. Yet, despite all of that, many of those months were the happiest of my
life, when I got to see how truly impassioned Ezra was for living, and when I got
to feel my greatest pride over the strong, resilient, gracious person he'd grown to be.*

   *"I grieve for my son daily, hourly. I miss his spark in my life, his clever way
with words and strange ideas. I miss Ezra constantly, as a dull, edgeless ache; but
cutting through that ache with sharp clarity is the pain and awe of the night he
died. So, in its way, I had been writing this poem in my head for three years.*

   *"My last words to him, as close as I can remember them, are in the poem,
and those too draw from the early days of his diagnosis, one of our tricks for
coping with IV placements and waves of headache pain. He died squeezing my
fingers, the first time in months that I'd asked him to give me his pain."*

   Chatterton's poems and essays have appeared in The Coachella Review,
Mosaic, Naranjas y Nopales, *and* Main Channel Voices. *He lives in Riverside,
California, and works as an elementary school librarian, "trying to teach
students to love words and paper as much as I do." He and his wife are "happily
expecting our first child together, my second son."*

LUCKY

by Lisa Robertson

Two parents
over two years
shared one oncologist
one hospital
one hospice
also the truncation
of two lives
I was still young
I did not feel lucky

Metastatic meningioma
and your distress over the loss
not of sight, motor skills, and language
but the ability to perform abstract calculations,
a magical math which gave you
pause and the suggestion
of a liminal world

And I am no help
the daughter of the entomologist cannot count
to forthcoming infinity
but no matter, you tell me
infinity is not found in the counting
only through the calculus
of inscrutable equations
on an infinite scale
can you count past one, you say?

I suggest that a character of Nabokov's said
life is nothing but a joke
but you say that jokes make us laugh
and so maybe Roethke got it right,
maybe we do end in joy

One: my greatest luck in life was to have been your daughter

And then outside the oncology wing window
a common house finch passes
not Flaubert's parrot of transcendence
but a moth-colored bird
wings striated as a Noctuidae moth
so out of season, to suggest escape of
a domestic prison
the workaday confinement, the tedium
the finch has ascended to this brand-new life
of the hospital courtyard

And you surprised me, when you said:
how lucky we are to see it, so late in the season

Two: that bird was another thing
And I look away, overwhelmed by all the ways we have been fortunate.

––––––––

Lisa Robertson's father and mother were both diagnosed with terminal cancer in their early sixties, dying in 2009 and 2010 respectively. "My parents were absolutely my best friends," says Robertson, thirty-eight. "I lost them to cancer, and so I find it strange, and maybe a bit of a betrayal, to say that cancer was a teacher, but it was.

"During the hardest time, when both of my parents were critically ill, when our household was full of bad news and dismal test results, my father, a biologist and naturalist, worried that his daughters would eventually see less beauty in the world. And while the world certainly was a darker place for a while, my sister and I were also left with the remainder of the small precious things our father took care to show us, even on the most shattering days.

"Cancer might try to convince you that anything can be lost, but my parents taught me that if you examine the natural world with a careful eye, any number of miracles can be found."

Robertson has worked in public health, biostatistics, and epidemiology for over a decade. She lives in the San Francisco Bay Area with her husband, a daughter — "a constant reminder of the things that my parents taught me" — a small dog, and a very large cat.

MOUNTAIN LAUREL

by Gary Hugh Fry

As dawn takes the last star
dimming in the pale silver sky
the blade of a faraway saw
rings clear and everlasting
remembrances rise unbidden
these are the faces of white
stones twinkling up
from a childhood stream

a small boy watches his father
charming mahogany into whirling
carbon steel dreams of a father
taming golden trout to the glittering
lure and dreams of a night long ago
when a boy and his father nestled
down in a tent pitched bravely
against the stars

I remember when my father's lungs
began to rattle like castanets in
the terrible wind of his cough
when his flesh dropped like
blossoms of mountain laurel
until the last white
petal fell away
to earth.

---

*Gary Fry, seventy-one, wrote this poem to honor his father, who died within five
months after his diagnosis with metastatic lung cancer. Fry's credits include poems,
book reviews, and essays published by the American Bar Association,
the Arizona Bar Association and small presses.*

 *Fry is a retired lawyer, who lives with his wife, Karen, and their motley pets on
a mammoth kill site in southeastern Arizona, just minutes from the Mexican border.*

MY FATHER'S SHIRTS

by Carrie Green

My father emptied his room the spring
he found out. *So your mother won't have to,* he said,
as he opened the metal doors of the closet
and rattled the quiet afternoon. He plucked shirts
from hangers and held them out to decide
which to toss and which to keep.

He'd paced all morning, needing to keep
himself busy. It was late spring,
but the magnolias hesitated, unable to decide
to unfurl. The doctor said
he still had time. There were so many shirts
packed inside my father's closet.

He stared into the open mouth of the closet
at all the clothes too big to keep:
pants that sagged and bunched, shirts
that swallowed him. The warm spring
sun filtered through leaves and blinds. He said,
It shouldn't be so hard to decide.

Why was it so hard to decide?
Birthdays, trips: all contained in his closet.
Your brother gave me this, he said
of a fishing shirt he wanted to keep.
My throat tight, forgetting spring,
I filled the bags with piles of shirts.

I pictured the bereft racks of thrift-store shirts
and knew my father was right to decide
now, when he could open the window to spring
and brighten the dim hole of his closet.
Still, I wanted him to keep
everything. *You might wear those again,* I said.

I'll never wear these again, he said,
holding up the blue work shirts
with *Gary* stitched in red. *We'll always keep
those,* I said. It was easy to decide
to put them back, safe inside his closet,
ready to be worn another spring.

He died the next spring. My mother said
it hurt to open his closet. We pressed his shirts
to our faces to decide what to keep.

———

Carrie Green, thirty-nine, started writing about her father about a year after his death from stage-four pancreatic cancer. "I didn't think I was ready to write about him, but one day as I was at my desk playing around with a writing exercise, out he came in a poem. Then another and another. These poems can be difficult to write, but at the same time, they make me feel close to my father."

Green's previously published credits include Cave Wall, The Louisville Review, The Pinch, *and other journals. She lives with her husband in Lexington, Kentucky, and works as a reference librarian in a public library.*

NATIVITY: FOUR MONTHS LATER

by Donna Isaac

why is it then that when I close my eyes I see not the baby
in the agrestic manger or the watery-eyed donkey by his side
nor the star that makes us shiver and cry out in joy

but a jamaican lady lifting my brother into a barred bed
just four months ago while he cried beneath an eye patch
and tried to look for jesus and justice in it all

or see another room when mama lay in silence
upon pure white sheets   breath pumped in   and
we, terrified, knew what we knew and fell to the floor

on broken knees not to a baby born but to souls flown away
my eyes clearly see the wrenched face   resigning will
he will not stay   no   longer a matter of if

mother, brother, are you there or here while
we walk among shadows stringing garland needling
cranberries popcorn and sit in spilled treelight

hearing a horned owl in the snow hooting outside showing
how to see how to go to how to swoop 'round
a golden godhead shining reminding   to touch

and play the strings of love   my violin
tucked beneath a chin wet with tears and though I tenderly
bow "o holy night"   this hand it trembles   trembles

Donna Isaac, fifty-eight, wrote this poem about her brother, Tommy, who died of nasopharyngeal cancer; it also references her mother, who passed away from leukemia. "The Christmas after Tommy's death... I could not embrace Christmas in a joyful way as I usually did. Jesus figures in the poem juxtaposed in his birth (in the manger) and in the allusion to trembling as is present in the old country hymn, 'Were You There When They Crucified My Lord?'"

Isaac's chapbooks include Tommy *and* Holy Comforter; *she also has poems in* The St. Paul Almanac, Hospital Drive, Perfect Dragonfly, *and others.*

A Virginia native, Isaac has taught English and writing for thirty-seven years; she has a Master of Fine Arts degree from Hamline University. She and husband Matt live in a suburb of St. Paul, Minnesota, on a pond where they enjoy wildlife, including deer, egrets, raccoons, and more.

ON THE DAY OF HER DIAGNOSIS
for my mother

by Barbara Crooker

a cold wind was bearing
down, straight from Canada.

The small pearl I'd seen floating
in the warm water of her breast

was cancer, a word that hissed
in the ear like fat in a pan

or the breath of a snake.
With these two syllables, the dice

rolled, and the odds went up
for all the women in my family.

Early November, most of October's
gold has fallen, bruise-colored clouds

moving in. I remember being six,
sick in bed, how the winter trees

scratched the leaden sky, witches in a Grimm
tale, how she brought me cinnamon

toast and milky tea. Now I bring her lentil
soup, with circles of kielbasa, carrots, onions;

scones warm from the oven, spread with strawberry
jam, whatever bit of sweetness I can scrape

from the jar. Mother, daughter, all the old stories,
the frost moon, the loss moon, sinking below the horizon.

———

Barbara Crooker's mother was in her late eighties when she was diagnosed with
cancer. When they learned that breast cancer is not likely to compromise health
in women over eighty-five, "the radiologist told us to go out for lunch, instead of
ever coming back to the hospital. Mom lived to celebrate her ninetieth birthday,
and this cancer was never a 'player.'" (On the Day of Her Diagnosis" was first
published in Dogwood.*)*

  Crooker, sixty-seven, has published fifteen collections of poetry. Her poems
have appeared in JAMA, The Green Mountains Review, The Potomac
Review, Good Poems for Hard Times *(Garrison Keillor, editor), and many*
other journals and anthologies.

  Crooker is a writer and full-time caregiver of a child (now twenty-eight)
with autism. She and her husband have two grown daughters, and three
adorable grandchildren. She lives and writes in rural northeastern Pennsylvania.

ONE SMALL PLEASURE

by Courtney E. Putnam

Today I am an alchemist, combining the ingredients
into a small glass bowl: sugar, dried rosemary leaves,
and peppermint with warm almond oil.
I roll my dad's khakis up to his knees,
and with a white towel under his legs to catch
the sprinkling of my exfoliant mixture, I softly scrub
the dry, scaly skin chemo has left.

He closes his eyes as I massage the mixture
from the bottom of his feet, circling up his shins and calves,
to his knees and back down again. With warm moist towels,
I wash away the excess and see his legs turn pink
and smooth. "Feel how soft they are, Dad," I say,
as he smiles and rubs his shins, then asks for more.

This is one small pleasure —
to be touched without latex gloves, skin to skin, sugar
and herbs instead of alcohol and iodine,
his own couch to sink into,
his wife nearby watching this experiment unfold,
and his daughter saying through her touch,
This is one thing I can do, Dad. This is at least one thing.

Courtney E. Putnam's father used to tell her, "Just love me." She did that "fiercely," she says. "But I also found that I could comfort my father with my skills as a bodywork practitioner. I gave him massage, Reiki, salt scrubs, and other healing, non-invasive touch to offset the often well-meaning, yet intrusive, procedures he had to endure for his cancer." Her father passed away just seven months after his diagnosis with stage-four kidney cancer.

Putnam's poems have been featured in 4th Street, Yours Truly, Phoebe, *and others.*

Putnam is a part-time healer and part-time artist living in Seattle, Washington. She has "a grounding significant other of eight years and a comforting ten-year-old cat."

PICKING OUT WIGS

by Gina Forberg

She wanted human hair, nothing synthetic, length short to medium. Her
head with its wisps and bald spots demanded a petite size, though my
mother had never been petite in anything her whole life.
I flipped through the wigs in the Raquel Welch/Hair-U-Wear collection —
"Courage," "Fortitude," Hope" — thinking these names alone might cure
her.
The mannequin heads fascinated me: fiberglass regular, fiberglass long
neck, fiberglass with arm. They even had a fiberglass afro, and all four
had life-like features — eyes, nose, mouth, even hand-decorated
eyelashes. A blank-faced Styrofoam one came free with the purchase
of a wig.
After hours in the shop, the table covered with glossy-print models, she
chose one perm, one feathered, one eighties-big-hair. She added a
rubber-grip wire brush, a two-way pick, shampoo and conditioner.
Back home, I lined up the Styrofoam mannequins on her dresser, the
backs of their naked heads reflected in the mirror, and gave each a
name: "Dream," "Embrace," "Real."

*Gina Forberg, forty-nine, credits reading "My Mother's Hair," a poem by Denise
Duhamel, for sparking this poem. "It reminded me of my mother during her
illness and how she insisted on having wigs, rather than go bald."*

Forberg's poems have appeared in Mochila Review, Slant Magazine,
Inkwell Magazine, *and numerous other literary journals.*

*Forberg is an elementary physical education teacher and lives in
Fairfield, Connecticut, with her son, Griffin. She is a student at The Writers
Studio in the advanced poetry class in New York City.*

PLENTY

by Elizabeth Batchelder

She lies there
asleep, sort of.
With the beat of the machines
keeping time
time
time.

Nurses come in,
check vitals, change bags,
measure pee.
Ask,
"Anything else you need?"

Yes, she thinks.
A little energy.
Food I can keep down.
Visitors who don't look so sad.
Not much.

Yes, she thinks.
Cocktails with friends.
Stress over finals.
A silly Facebook status.
My life back.

Yes, she thinks.
To hear my parents laugh again.
To watch my brother grow up.
To travel the Mediterranean.
To finish a triathlon.

A lover. Babies.
A house by the water.
My chance to make a difference.
More time.

Yes, she thinks.
A cure that is not so fucking violent.
So ravaging. So tenuous.
Fifty more years.
Plenty.

"No thanks," she says.
"I'm good."

Elizabeth Batchelder's stepdaughter — "she really is a daughter to me" — was twenty-six when she was diagnosed with stage-four neuroblastoma, a disease usually found in young children. Today she is in partial remission, has completed her master's degree in social work, is in love, and is working as a pediatric oncology social worker.

"I am not generally a person who writes poetry," says Batchelder, fifty-two. "But that day, watching Chelsea trying to express basic needs to her nurses, I pulled a piece of paper out of my bag, wrote 'Plenty' and felt, somehow, that I brought her voice out." This is her first published poem.

Batchelder is a retired bank executive. She, husband Doug, and their crazy dogs live in Spokane, their adopted hometown. They are new grandparents to Calliope Elizabeth.

The Cancer Poetry Project 2

A POEM FOR JOHN

by Kathleen Hayes Phillips

Tonight I wrestle snakes,
stuff them into a bag, throw
the squirming bundle
over my shoulder
and head for the roof,
down long passages
no map
deadends
and the floodwaters
rising.

Mother told me to keep you safe
and I can't.

Now it is time to get up
sit in the kitchen
and wait for day
when normal comes,
the grind of the school bus
an early crow and angry jay.
I can bake cookies,
Mom's frosted ones
you love.

You still have your appetite
and your hair,
but I know I must hurry.
We still might outrun the flood
and I know Mother's directions
by heart.

Kathleen Hayes Phillips, seventy-seven, still misses her brother, John, who died at sixty-nine from lung and bone cancer.

Phillips started writing poetry about twenty years ago "to understand what is happening in my life." Her poetry has been published in Free Verse, Siftings from the Clearing, Hummingbird, *and other journals. Her poems have also appeared in the following anthologies:* Cradle Songs, Love Over Sixty, Verse and Vision, *and* The Clearing Speaks. *She has published seven chapbooks of her own poetry.*

Phillips is a wife of fifty-one years, mother of four, and grandmother of four. She is a retired teacher and religious education director. She and her husband recently moved from their home of thirty-five years to an apartment in Milwaukee.

THE QUILT MAKER

by Bill Carpenter

All her life she made quilts,
sewing cloth into patterns,
to give away at weddings,
showers and christenings.
Mapping her family history:
a small blue-and-white collage
of triangles and squares
tells of the birth of a baby boy;
a large green wreath
encircling a rose mosaic,
the marriage of a second cousin.
Her craft warms as it inspires,
reminds as it delights,
spread in a grid of connections
across the globe:
one hangs in an Irish monastery,
another blankets a teacher
sleeping on a futon in Tokyo.

Even after doctors embossed
a wedge of scar tissue
across her chest,
she continued
stitching her heart
into a comforter for a loved one.
And when they returned
with more cuts and grafts,
leaving her skin
a patchwork of sutured flesh,
even then, sitting in the shadow,

she sewed
parcels of cloth
into a tightly knit overlay of relations
giving herself completely
to the art of quilt making.

Bill Carpenter, sixty-seven, wrote this poem about his cousin who died of breast cancer. "I was inspired to write this poem because of Marcia's irrepressible selflessness in the face of death," Carpenter says. "Her life was a gift to everyone who knew her. She was the kind of person who restores your belief in our capacity for love and generosity."

Carpenter's publishing credits include Surrounded: Living with Islands, Origami Poets Project, Tiferet, *and many others.*

Carpenter is a retired rehabilitation counselor and supervisor who lives in Chepachet, Rhode Island, with his partner, Emily. He has four adult children and one grandchild, and he looks after his mother who turned ninety last year. He is a member of the Ocean State Poets, whose mission is to bring poetry and give voice to nontraditional populations, such as prisoners and nursing home residents.

The Cancer Poetry Project 2

RISING CANCER

by Susannah Gilbert

*You are dreamy, with a
psychological nature that is
oriented toward nostalgia for things past,
toward your mother and your family.*
— *Taurus Rising Cancer description*

Sometimes,
I dream about the future,
about hospital rooms.
When I wake, I touch my stomach
searching for the scars that
appeared in the dream,
where I saw myself dissected.

My future is dictated by a
50/50 coin flip.
I didn't fail statistics;
I know how it goes.

I close my eyes and
the hospital rooms of the past,
the waiting rooms of my childhood,
meld with the operating rooms of my adulthood.
I am marooned between nostalgia and fear of the unknown,
in these amorphous years
of knowing and waiting.

Susannah Gilbert, twenty, is a Taurus, rising Cancer, which inspired this poem about the limbo between genetic testing for Lynch Syndrome and an actual cancer diagnosis. She has watched her mother deal with four separate Lynch cancers, and is fascinated by the differences and similarities between being a family member, patient, and future patient. "I have always written both fiction and poetry," says Gilbert, "so writing about cancer was a logical choice when trying to work through all of this. My mother is also a poet and writer and has written a lot of poetry about her journey, encouraging me to do the same."

Gilbert is a junior at Lawrence University in Appleton, Wisconsin, majoring in English and religious studies.

SAYING HELLO TO GOODBYE

by Veneta Masson

We don't know how it will end
but this is how it begins —
two sisters alone
sitting like tailors
with dinner on trays
        mostly untouched.

But it doesn't run in the family
we say in turn
then laugh till we cry
for now we know that
any improbable thing
        can happen

like losing a breast in the morning.
The spring twilight lingers on
while we drain our wine glasses
glad to be tipsy
saying hello
        to goodbye.

---

*This is one of more than thirty poems that Veneta Masson, sixty-eight, wrote
about her younger sister, Rebecca, and her life with breast cancer. "It was purely
by chance that I was visiting her when she received her cancer diagnosis, and
pure gift that we were able to share much of the journey that profoundly affected
both our lives. 'Saying Hello' began to form in my mind soon after that evening
we spent alone in her bedroom, oblivious to the sounds of a bustling household
just outside the shut door."*

Masson's most recent collection of poetry, Clinician's Guide to the Soul, *is
meant for family caregivers as well as health professionals. She is a family nurse
practitioner and writer living in Washington, D.C. Although she is no longer in
practice, she teaches a course in health-care ethics at Georgetown University.*

SIDE BY SIDE

by Kari O'Driscoll

Wide opaque circles of Turtle Wax
dry on the hood of Dad's car on a hot Saturday morning.
Swirls barely overlap,
concentric circles like 45s of the Kingston Trio.

We work side by side,
me silent,
loathe to break the spell and remind him that I am not a son.
His deep metronomic voice teaches me how to polish just so:
"Leave no trace."
"Any job worth doing is worth doing perfectly."

I could never be his son.
But as Dad lay dying,
cancer silently stalking his healthy cells with reckless abandon,
I was the one strong enough to admit it to.

Everyone else heard the brave mantras:
"I'm fighting this thing hard."
"I'll beat this."

We sit side by side.
He is silent,
unwilling to break the spell as I rub swirls of lotion on his dry forearms.
Just so.

Kari O'Driscoll, forty-one, "worshipped my father as a child, vilified him as a teen, and had a hard time coming to terms with the fact that he was allowed to be human until I got pregnant with my first daughter and experienced firsthand what it meant to be a parent. We began anew, building our relationship as adults with mutual respect and had eight glorious years as father and daughter before he died. The poems I wrote are about coming full circle in our relationship and reveling in the simple moments we had together."

O'Driscoll has written essays for BuddhaChick Magazine and has had work syndicated on BlogHer.com. She lives with her husband and "two lovely daughters" in the beautiful Pacific Northwest; the family enjoys spending time together reading, playing games, and exploring their neighborhood.

SLEEP TROUBLE

by Amy Marengo

Somewhere in that building
my niece makes herself small
in a narrow bed, unfolding
pink-and-blue-striped newborn
blankets on each pillow. She sweats
poison into the sea of little blankets.

Somewhere in that building
at least one mother is crying quietly
enough not to wake her baby.
One time a mother's cry woke the whole ward
when she found her baby wasn't breathing.

My sister said she spent the rest
of the night nuzzling her daughter's
bald head and watching the port jerk up
and down on her chest — she
said she doesn't believe in God,
but when that mother screamed
for everyone — anyone — to pray, she did.

---

*Amy Marengo, twenty-seven, "felt compelled to write a poem about what I find
to be an overlooked corner of society: sick children and their parents who struggle
to live day by day, sometimes hour by hour, behind hospital walls." Marengo
understands this reality firsthand: Her niece, Malia, was diagnosed with
stage-four neuroblastoma in 2011, endured fourteen months of treatments,
and in July 2012, was declared to have "no evidence of disease."*

Marengo's poetry has appeared in Poetry Quarterly, Pressed Wafer, Inman
Review, *and other journals. She works for MaliaCrushesCancer.com, her family's
nonprofit, and is pursuing a Master of Fine Arts degree in poetry at Virginia Tech.*

S'MORE

by Megan Willome

On a cool August evening in the San Juan Mountains,
we gathered around a chiminea to make s'mores.

Chocolate and graham crackers were no match
for our family's flaming marshmallows.

The kids shouted how best to roast puffed sugar.
We smushed sticky fingers into the bag

grabbed our prey
perfected our technique

poked sticks into the fire over and over again.
"We should sing, 'Kumbaya,'" said Mom.

We all laughed.
It didn't seem like a time for camp songs.

We needed sweet summer blues
during this, our last, vacation together.

Mom reached her stick into the flames,
her short, marshmallow hair bleached white

by chemo. The fire of her cancer contained,
for now,

in a vessel we could still jab
with prayers,

devouring each bright moment,
as if her bag of marshmallows would never run out.

Megan Willome, forty-two, wrote this poem about her mother, who was diagnosed with breast cancer in 1981 and lived with multiple metastes for nearly thirty years. When cancer returned in her liver, Willome wrote more than seventy poems about the experience. "Why not write about cancer?" she asks. "It's got the two great themes — love and death. Plus, it helped me to get through those last two years by knowing that every moment we still had was a cherished moment. I didn't want to forget anything."

Willome is a contributing writer and managing editor of the Wacoan *magazine, a lifestyle magazine published in Waco, Texas. She has had five poems featured in Tweetspeak Poetry's "Every Day Poems." Willome is married, has two teenagers, and lives in Fredericksburg, Texas.*

SOME THOUGHTS YOU MIGHT HAVE
TWENTY MINUTES AFTER YOUR GRANDFATHER
HAS DIED

by Manda Frederick

1.

When you kiss the corpse
that is your grandfather,

he is cool as fruit, you think,
and your first impulse is to warm

him — draw up his hospital quilt,
rub your palm where the pulse

is strong in his wrist,
encourage his blood flowing.

2.

The stillest your father has ever been
is in that blind he built

with his dad — any movement,
even slight, would petrify the prey

he seeks to kill. Any sound
or scent, and those deer transfix

and listen, gauge the strength
of what it is that moves — his heart.

They wait to hear it until the chill
is black and they know his line of sight

is stretched too thin to follow home.
And they wait for him to rise; they can

see him now — he is just a man. He is cold
and weak; they can see that now.

3.

There are some words that mean
nothing until they come to you —

denotation materialized: Grief.
You speak it sentence-less,

and it creates in you an arousal
of damage — this word, how you

sound it out, feel it rooted wrongly
in your neck as cancer of the throat.

Grief is in your father's face;
you can see that now. You imagine

your own face takes the shape
of fear. You fear your parents' death.

And, now, you can see what you fear —
how it has a beginning. How it has begun.

4.

You think of that last winter your father
helped you dig, the work of plows

undone, the shoveled-out mounds
of snow amassed at the edges

of your lot. You adapted your simple
soft-suited form to disappear

into the den your father made, the mitten-
punched dome, dissolving cathedral

of dirt and ice. You feared the engines
that steered the corners of your cave,

the boot ridges kicking down, the blade-slick
sleds. You feared your father could not

see you. That he would forget you there,
leave you blinking darkly into the threat of collapse.

*Manda Frederick is an assistant professor of writing arts at Rowan University,
Glassboro, New Jersey. She is also editor-in-chief of* Glassworks, *a magazine of
literature and art. She has published poetry, fiction, and nonfiction in a number
of journals, and she's "happy to be honoring the memory of her grandfather."*

TONIC WATERS

by Susan Bernardo

She wakes from a nap on the sofa.
It is late afternoon. She wants a cocktail.
I offer other tonics — a cup of tea, soft music, conversation.
She stares out the window at the East River,
a slow barge is making its way west.
"Looks like the water's flowing backwards," I say.
She tells me it is tidal, the ocean pushing back against
the river currents, muddying the water at the juncture.
I offer to rub her back, ease her pain.
She struggles to find a comfortable position.
fingers the device at her chest, where once she cradled my husband.

They call it a port, but really it is a canal.
The Suez, the Panama — channels cut by men into the verdant land
to ferry their loads of lumber and steel, coffee and chemicals.
A thousand upon a thousand laborers leveled the boulders,
dug the trenches, laid the steel. Left their families behind
to seek a living, their hopeful letters home slowing, ceasing.
In an instant, earth can swallow our engineering marvels
crumble them to dust, surge over us in a great wash
while we stand with our finger in the dam.

I whisper my hands across the relief map that is her spine,
navigating the ridges and deep valleys.
the lotion disappears into her deflated skin like
water from a canteen spilling onto parched earth.
I want her to be a leaf floating on the water.
I want her to be a drop lifted from the sea, vaporous,
before she rains to earth again.

When Susan Bernardo's mother-in-law, Loretta, was diagnosed with a rare form of stomach cancer, "I felt overwhelming sadness that my elegant mother-in-law — who loved her gin-and-tonic-before-dinner ritual — was suffering so much," she says. "But as we sat there watching the river flow in front of us, there was also a certain beauty in the moment. In her vulnerability, I felt bonded to her on a deeper level than ever before. It was a gift to be with her, and I wanted to pay tribute to that." Loretta died in 2009, within a year of her diagnosis.

Bernardo, forty-five, authored a children's book, Sun Kisses, Moon Hugs, "born out of a desire to comfort children dealing with loss and separation anxiety." She holds a bachelor's degree in English from UCLA and a master's degree in English literature from Yale. She also facilitates creativity workshops and stays in touch "with my inner flower child by dancing, raising cats and chickens, sculpting, painting, tide pooling, and taking nature hikes with my two amazing sons." She lives in Encino, California.

TOUCH ME

by Janine Soucie Kelley

You tell your lover

the long thin scar
dividing your skin
into hemispheres
tattoos the memory of a trip
down the Amazon
where you met
a strange tribe of healers
whose ceremonies
and rites of passage
tested your courage and faith
teaching you a new language.

You faced
the dark night of the soul
the white day with its blind stars
searching for the hidden face of God
near the fabled healing rivers of love
whose Beatitudes wash away
anger and fear.
You left this rainforest of suffering
naked, new-born
an explorer discovering
how to love this new body
how to map its scars into beauty

how to say, *Touch me, Touch me here.*

At age thirteen, Janine Soucie Kelley's daughter was diagnosed with ovarian cancer; she is "now radiantly athletic, a vegan, and cancer free more than a decade later." Kelley wrote this poem to honor her daughter's "resilience, beauty and courage" and to inspire other cancer survivors to "love and accept their brave new bodies."

Kelley's publishing credits include a novel, A Window Girl of Amsterdam, *and poems in many journals, including* Calyx *and* The Salt River Review. *She is an award-winning poet and playwright, and has taught English, theater, journalism, and creative writing in diverse schools and colleges in the Southwest. An amateur astronomer and avid hiker, she lives in Arizona with her husband. Her son and daughter are pursuing their dreams and happiness in Hollywood.*

UNBEARABLE BRIGHTNESS OF HAIR

by David Sten Herrstrom

Nothing lets go all at once
  not love, and least the hair.
   Chemicals course her veins

swifter than bloodhounds,
  indiscriminately scorch
   cancer cells and follicles.

Yet death does not reach the tips
  of hair for weeks. They glint
   like waves of sunlit wheat.

In the basement of her body
  she waits with cricket chirps
   of silence and certainty

and signs plain as a muffled boom
  exploding in the sultry distance —
   some strands alive on her plate

the bright web on her pillow.
  She dreams a mangy dog,
   fur islands on raw pink

then wakes with her hand grazing
  her head, unawares,
   and coming back like a hound

with its mouth of feathers. Her cry
  is silent, but her lover wakes,
   his hair a fountain beside her.

He holds her like one drowning
 surrounded by the brightness.
  She breathes again. He lets go

slowly and returns quickly
 from the bathroom, head shaved
  bare as a bulb, as if to say

there's no excuse but love.

---

*David Sten Herrstrom, wrote this poem in honor of his daughter, Tristen.
"I attempted to find language for the dread that my daughter experienced
'in the basement of her body,' seeing signs of the onslaught of poisons attacking
her cancer cells," he says. "[The poem] also celebrates a friend's faithfulness
and courage."*

Herrstrom's publications include the textbook, Writing as Discovery;
Jonah's Disappearance, *a sequence of poems with drawings by Jacob Landau;*
"A Sonata for J.S. Bach," *a collaboration with composer Laurie Altman;
and the libretto for* The Outlaw and the King. *His poems have appeared in*
Columbia, US1 Worksheets, Nimrod, *and more. He also has received a
poetry fellowship from the New Jersey State Council on the Arts and has
been nominated for a Pushcart Prize. Herrstrom has a doctorate in English
literature from New York University. He and his wife, Constance Joy, live in
Roosevelt, New Jersey.*

UNCOVERED

by Cynthia Rausch Allar

I prayed for months to Anthony, the patron
saint of all things lost, to return the lace
mantilla — white-thread netting interwoven
with roses, pearl-like beads — that I'd worn to Mass
each Sunday. I prayed and waited, in a sort
of test. What sort of saint would deny the devout
request of a child? To look grown up, I'd worn
this pretty bit of veil. It wasn't about
vanity. I knew nothing of vanity
at twelve. A few months later, my prayer was answered.
The lost mantilla was sent back, but the rules
had changed by then. The church was letting girls
and women go to Mass with heads uncovered.
It came too late. I thanked St. Anthony.

In a hospital named for him, my mother died
the next year. They found the tumor, interwoven
threads in the grey matter of comprehension.
Too late. Through radiation treatments, I prayed,
through nausea, pleurisy, mother's head uncovered
twice, by surgery, by cell death. White
knit cap to try to hide the scars, scarlet
monk's hood to ward against the chill of winter.
They hid her naked pain from those who could not
bear it. My fingers interlaced the rosary —
beads, pearl-white knuckles. *Holy Mary,*
mother of God... she died by spring. By God,
I grew up then. And with my first black dress,
I wore the white mantilla to her last Mass.

Cynthia Rausch Allar, fifty-six, wrote this poem about her mother, who was diagnosed with brain cancer in 1968 and died six months later when Allar was thirteen. "They say writers each have their own obsession, which appears in their writing over and over," *she says.* "For many years, mine was my mother and her death. Writing about it has helped me to grieve and to accept dying as a part of life. I also believe poetry to be a way to share hard-earned wisdom with our fellow human beings."

Allar's poems have appeared in Future Eyes, Naugatuck River Review, *and* Off the Rocks, *among others. Her essay,* "'A Snake Lies Hid:' Aphra Behn's Poetry and the War Between the Sexes," *appeared in* Allegorica.

Allar is a transplant to Pasadena, California, where she lives with her wife, whom she met in the Spalding Master of Fine Arts in Writing program.

WAITING

by J. Anna Michaelis

we wait
in tight, airless rooms
with stark walls as fifty-gallon
fish tanks take up our worry space
we become light headed & batty
as the last bits of rationed oxygen
drain into our nervous, shallow lungs
we wait for doctors to finally tell us
the answer, for our faces to cease
creasing with worry, for platelets in thin
hollow curves of transparency to be invited
into the flow, for saline to plop one last
drop down a narrow plastic channel
we wait for television shows to cycle,
for nurses to restock the floor's kitchen with sweet
hits of cellophane-swathed Lorna Doones dipped in
tiny peanut butter tubs to offer
a stolen moment of bliss in hallway silence
stabbed by staccato machine blips & bleeps
we wait for blue vinyl wheelchairs to taxi us
down to another procedure where we sit
in rigid, Scotch-guarded chairs & stare
at patterns in tight-knit carpet until
our fluorescent fatigued eyes cross &
surgeons in an azure blur of
clogs & scrubs enter & hover with lips
synching up with the news
we wait to hear
we at last
are released.

J. Anna Michaelis, twenty-six, lost her brother, Ryan, at age fourteen to acute lymphocytic leukemia; she was nine years old.

"So many years have passed since my brother was ill that it has started to feel like it was a past life, like maybe it hadn't even happened to me, and I was starting to forget the details," says Michaelis. "I felt like I needed to reclaim those extremely formative years, tap into all of those intense sensory experiences that had settled to the bottom of my memory, and create something with all of the energy that has been hibernating with those experiences." One result is this poem.

Michaelis has enjoyed publication previously in Summit Avenue Review. *She lives in "a cozy apartment" in St. Paul, Minnesota, and works as a barista at an independent coffee shop. "I keep company with a feisty bunny named Ollie and love writing with fountain pens."*

WHAT THEY'LL KNOW

by Paula Finn

My sister takes a rock
shaped like her missing breast
and carries it up the mountain
soaked in every color of the fall.
She lodges the rock
between a maple's forking roots
where it will last longer, I know,
than either of us.
From there, she can see
the hunkered backs of the Catskills
and the sun sending its coral lineaments
arcing through the dusk.
Later, she'll wake her small boys in the dark,
load them into a wheelbarrow
and push them back up the mountain.
They will know nothing of the rock,
yet something of this woman with one breast
who rouses them from sleep
to watch meteor showers
pouring into predawn.

Paula Finn, dedicates "What They'll Know" to her sister, who, as a mother of two young children, was diagnosed with breast cancer. Ten years hence, her sister and her family continue to live in "the light and shadows of the Catskills."

Finn's writing includes a chapbook, Eating History *(Finishing Line Press). She has published her work in journals and wrote the poetry for the award-winning dramatic oratorio,* From the Fire. *A graduate of the New York University Poetry program, Finn lives in Malawi with her husband and two sons.*

WITNESS

by Stacy R. Nigliazzo

Portal of flesh
perched just above the left breast —

better for chemotherapy
since her veins *like to blow.*

Surgically placed three days prior.

He rifles through the chart, strips away
the spent gauze.

Are you gonna do my head shunt, too? she whispers.
They say it's in the brain now.

He does not reply.

Scribbles a few hurried lines.
Closes the door.

In the mid-fourteenth century, doctors walked the streets
in waxen coats — observed the masses

from behind masks shaped like birds' beaks.
Stuffed the tips with flowers and spices

so as not to smell the afflicted.
Wielded wooden sticks to prod away the dying,

lest they be touched.

The window
above her bed overlooks a bustling courtyard.

Blackbirds on the slanted sill
roost in nests of scattered refuse —

whistle elegies and lullabies.

---

*"My mother's death from acute myeloid leukemia was unexpectedly quick
and is an experience I will never forget," says Stacy R. Nigliazzo, thirty-nine.
"I find especially memorable the exchanges with her providers of care. Most were
incredibly positive. Her oncologist was patient and kind, and the nurse who
cared for her on the night she died was truly an angel for both of us.*

*"But there were the inevitable exceptions. One surgeon, in particular,
stands out as an unfortunate example of a terrible bedside manner.... He simply
ignored her. I was angry at first, then I almost pitied him. Surely, such apathy
is not so far removed from misery. This poem is my reflection of that experience
and, hopefully, also serves as a lesson to any care providers who happen to read it.
Shortly after my mother died, I enrolled in nursing school and presently work
as an ER nurse. Ten years later, it is still a lesson for me."*

Nigliazzo's work has been featured in JAMA, the Annals of Emergency
Medicine, Third Space, *and the* Yale Journal for Humanities in Medicine,
among other publications. She also reviews poetry for the Bellevue Literary
Review *and the* American Journal of Nursing, *and is also a frequent
contributor. She lives in Humble, Texas.*

YET THERE IS STILL SUCH BEAUTY

by Jennifer Freed

There was your mother,
her birdlike chest the only one I ever knew,
and so I did not think it strange
to rest my head upon the hardness of her ribs
when she and Grandpa cuddled me in bed, and I delighted
in the small round pillows, so deliciously
resilient, that she lay on her bureau every night
for morning placement in her bra.

There was your friend, Kana, whose watercolor painting
of a frog, wearing a beret and standing at an easel,
you hung in your studio, to remind you
of her quiet whimsy,
and of the day she let you see her
hatless, scarfless, wigless,
let you wash the baby wisps of her once-thick hair,
and closed her eyes
and smiled
beneath your touch.

There was Karen, whose daughter, five years old,
you walked home from her first day of school,
she buoyant and abrim with happy chatter, for she did not understand
the meaning of her mother's weakness,
and still did not, at the burial,
where she ran off and twirled among the gravestones,
braids flying outward,
waiting for the somber-faced adults to notice
the glory of the bright blue day, of maple leaves, red and orange,
floating to her outstretched hands.

And there was you
in your late-summer garden on the day we brought you home,
your surgery not stopping you
from gently pulling weeds.
Your straw hat was tied beneath your chin, your shirt a vivid
pink, the sun slanting at the perfect angle
so that every blossom seemed lit from within — aster, sedum,
blanketflower, hosta —
and the light fell on your skin and, when you turned, it found your face
and you, like flowers,
were aglow.

Jennifer Freed, forty-seven, wanted to write something to commemorate the twenty years her mother has lived beyond breast cancer — years during which her mother has been her support and best friend. "If she'd not survived, she'd not have helped me plan a wedding, not have known the man I married, not have held or spoken with or been loved by her two granddaughters. What a wonderful thing, to have her still."

Two memories her mother shared of friends who hadn't survived breast cancer gave Freed "my way into the poem — that sense of beauty, in spite of everything." This is Freed's first published poem; previously, her poems "only lived in spiral notebooks, which I showed to no one. The Cancer Poetry Project's call for submissions gave me a reason to take out what I've written, clean it up, be brave enough to let others see." She lives with her husband and two daughters in central Massachusetts.

POEMS BY FRIENDS AND HEALTH ADVISORS

AFTER CANCER

by Mary Fitzpatrick

As I stand folding clothes
before going to bed
your pinched face is very near: white
mask, eyes buttoned
shut. My arms
know this work: dryer static
lifts my hair and the clothes
cling to me. The burnt
notion of our marriage has been annealed
by cancer's fires: spinal blaze,
lurid flowering cell-hater. I smooth
each arm down
to the body of shirt; pants are a pair
and the two legs meet. Socks, innocuous,
and underwear — with yours
I'll dust tables we fought over.
I'll be the widow and greet old friends
at funeral, burial, wake.
I'll be carried high
until all that's over, ever
in the service of your love.
You needed me more
when the back pain grew: couldn't stand up,
couldn't lie down. My dear,
your body (the pilot's arms I fell for),
the body of our love, is shrunken, racked and tested.
More ethereal now, our love —
late at night, folding electric clothes before bed
— stands on its own two feet.

Mary Fitzpatrick, fifty-eight, was inspired to write this poem by the cancer experience of family friends. "I loved the patient and his family — he and his wife were like an uncle and aunt to me. I imagined how her life would go on, raising three young children, and how the sense of his presence would not leave her for a long time."

Fitzpatrick says she writes poetry "for the same reasons we write about any intense experience that unites us, confounds us, and that must be processed to demonstrate compassion."

Previously published credits include North American Review; The Dos Passos Review; ASKEW, The Georgetown Review; *and the anthology,* A Bird Black as the Sun.

Fitzpatrick lives with her husband in Pasadena, California, the town in which she grew up and where she works as a communications manager in a large corporation.

AFTER CHEMO

by Ronald W. Pies

Come you home now, Love:
    Come you home
to bless our bed.
    Grace me
with the scent
    of your jasmined hair
and leave behind
    the bare stench
of chemistry.
    Come you home,
and let me
    pamper you
with strawberries.
    Leave behind
harsh latex
    and burning needles:
sweeten your tongue
    with coriander.
Come you home,
    and be lovely
in your battered bones,
    and let the doctors
not singe again
    your sullen marrow.
Come now, Love,
    and warm our bed,
and be
    the living border
against
    the quickening dead.
Come home now
    and let me rub you
with oil
    of sandalwood.

"*Many of my friends and family members have been stricken by cancer, including my father, who died of renal cancer when I was about seventeen*," *says Ronald W. Pies, M.D., sixty. This poem, he says, was influenced by the death of a good friend of his wife, after a long struggle with myelodysplastic disorder.*

"As a physician, I deal with 'disorders,'" he continues. "As a poet, I deal with 'disorder,' and writing poetry provides, in Robert Frost's words, 'a momentary stay against confusion.'"

Pies' poems have been published in The Literary Review, The Connecticut River Review, JAMA, *and several anthologies, including* Beyond Forgetting: Poetry and Prose about Alzheimer's Disease.

Pies is a psychiatric physician affiliated with SUNY Upstate Medical University and Tufts University. He lives outside of Boston with his wife, Nancy Butters. His interests include religion, philosophy, literature, and history.

BECAUSE

by Gail Carson Levine

Of course it's a snap for me to remember
that you wore a sweater but no coat because
the day was warm. You were tired, as usual,

and you didn't ask how I was doing, as usual,
or, by five minutes after I left, remember
what I wore or what the weather was, because

of the tumor and the slow diagnosis and because
of your wrecked brain and just because. The usual
disaster. Next time, again you won't remember,

but I'll remember, just because I can. The usual.

---

*When Gail Carson Levine's poetry teacher assigned a tritina, this is the poem
that came to her, inspired by a friend's experience with a brain tumor caused by
non-Hodgkin's lymphoma. "She's in remission — alive and kicking hard — but
was left with a brain injury and a lot of memory loss," says Levine, sixty-five.*

*"Poetry carries emotion more than any other kind of writing," she says,
"and cancer is freighted with feeling. I love to read and write poems. Writing
them helps me both know what I'm feeling and experience my sadness."*

*Levine is the author of twenty children's books, among them a poetry
collection called* Forgive Me, I Meant to Do It. *Her best-known book is the
children's novel* Ella Enchanted. *Her poems for adults have appeared in*
The Louisville Review, The Sugar House Review, *and an anthology of short
poems,* Bigger Than They Appear.

*Levine lives in a house built in 1790 in Brewster, New York, with her
husband, David, and Airedale Reggie.*

BREAKFAST

by Judith Goedeke

the sky simply wandered away
the trees and stones walked off
when he said cancer
I started living in a nightgown
feeling like a nuclear test site
exploded, toxic, uninhabitable
they arrived with bowls and bags and bottles
elbowed in and commandeered the kitchen
rifled through drawers and cabinets
figured out how to get the music going
tossed golden herb-laced quiche onto the table
alongside a rainbow of glistening fruit salad
a basket of bagels and satiny cream cheese
slivers of smoked salmon surrounded by satellites
of onion, capers, tomatoes and chopped egg
Gloria Estefan sang "Abriendo Puertas" through bursts of laughter
forks and knives clacked like snare drums
somebody put a mimosa in my hand, a whole strawberry perched on the glass
I was big as Michelin Man in my fuzzy bathrobe with stars and moons
holding that flute of effervescent sunshine, sipping tickly sweetness
the extravagant luxury of it, in my mouth
there is no stopping it
no matter how ghastly, nothing stands a chance
against love

When Judith Goedeke, fifty-nine, was diagnosed with kidney cancer, it left her "reeling, shell-shocked." That's when her friends arrived. "I'll never forget that day," she says. "They showed me I wasn't dead yet and taught me to keep finding simple pleasures no matter what." She calls this poem a thank-you to them. Since then, she says, a radical nephrectomy left her "well in all respects except one."

Now Goedeke's days are simpler and more restful — especially since scaling back her acupuncture practice to dedicate herself to writing. Her work has appeared in anthologies, Life in Me Like Grass on Fire *and* Dare to Repair.

She lives in a posh tree house in Laurel, Maryland, with her ever-curious engineer husband, Charlie.

BREAST CANCER SURVIVORS:
WRITING WORKSHOP, ONE THURSDAY NIGHT
AT BURGER KING

by Jeanne Bryner

Because we'd been locked out of the art gallery
(a sculptor forgot to leave the key she'd slipped into her purse),
I say, maybe we should cancel class. (November, six women
huddled in one car, our breath steaming windows like we're
cooking soup). No, no, no. They chant it like a song rehearsed;
we've done our homework. Okay, I say, but where? Someone
says, Burger King. We laugh. Okay, meet you there.
At first, the corner booth reminds me of crows, back-and-forth
catcalls, seven kids from *I don't give a shit* high school,
skull tattoos, spike dog collars, blue hair, every phrase
laced with *fuck* and *bitch*. I'm the workshop teacher.
I am well and start to wonder if what we're watching
might be the end product of a terrible experiment;
mold bubbling up from having it your way.
We get in line, buy our coffees. Two of the women smoke.
Class begins the old way, my tape recorder hums piano music,
ocean spray against some shore, slow deep breaths.
Spiral notebooks open hymnals in our laps. And I like
how one woman gives her husband hell (roses sent
first time, after her breast was removed), how another tells her kids not to
be afraid in foster care, she hopes they'll soon sleep under one roof.
And God, well She's afternoon-turn shift leader in a hairnet dressed like
somebody's mom who'd really be pretty if She had teeth. She's barking
orders to the grunts in back and listening very carefully
to the real deal, the *no happy meals sold here* poets,
Their journal entries stab of biopsy needles, the physics and bullshit of
lugging a case of Ensure up two flights
of stairs, outside apartment, winter's ice,
letters to lost breasts, shock of being bald,
endless puking after chemo.

You might not believe this, but those kids in the corner booth?
They disappeared.
I don't know when, but this really happened, just ask God.

Jeanne Bryner, sixty-one, wrote this poem about the women in her breast cancer survivors' writing workshop. "They were all survivors at different stages of the journey — all but two of them are still alive," she says. "I was moved to write the poem, because they insisted we still have class, even though we had to create a new space to do so. And it all went off without a hitch."

Her books in print are Breathless; Blind Horse: Poems; Eclipse: Stories; Tenderly Lift Me: Nurses Honored, Celebrated and Remembered; No Matter How Many Windows; The Wedding of Miss Meredith Mouse; _and_ Smoke: Poems, _which received second place in 2012 American Journal Book of the Year Awards._

Bryner has been a practicing registered nurse for over three decades and now works at Vlad Pediatrics. She lives in Newton Falls, Ohio.

CANCER, FOR DICKIE

by Cathy Barber

If you've seen a zodiac,
you know. Cancer is the crab.
From the Greek, *carcinos* for crayfish.
Hippocrates, premier coiner,
used the term even then for ulcers and growths.
Later, the Romans translated *carcinos* to cancer.
What an odd juxtaposition of meanings,
those tiny creatures and tinier menaces.

I used to catch crayfish in a clear stream
that ran under a narrow, metal bridge.
My sister, a few years older, and me,
in our childhood shorts. Jars in hand. The trick
was to scoop quick and deep with the jar.
The water sploshed as the jar broke
the surface. That method worked
for the first crayfish. I can't remember
how we got the rest. We must have rooted them out
by hand, moving their hiding places, the small rocks.

They were such scuttlers! Fast!
And they wiggled their tails in the bottom sand,
as though it were a blanket or living tissue
that would settle back over them.
We didn't keep them. We emptied our jars
in the stream.

I'd throw them back now if I could,
I'd throw them all back.

Cathy Barber, fifty-nine, didn't know how to help her friend, Dickie, who had been diagnosed with carcenoid tumors. "But, of course, I couldn't. So I did what I know how to do: write."

"Cancer, for Dickie" first appeared in The Bohemian, *the literary journal of Notre Dame de Namur in Belmont, California. Other poems and stories of Barber's have appeared in* Tattoo Highway, The Rio Grande Review, *and* The Dos Passos Review.

Barber is enrolled in the Master of Fine Arts program at the Vermont College of Fine Arts. In addition to writing poetry, she writes a humor blog. She lives with her husband in San Mateo, California.

CLINICAL OBSERVATIONS

by Max Money

A large aquarium sits in the lobby.
Three piles of melded coral and deep-pitted
purple rocks rest on a bed of white shells.
Several thin, shaded fish glide through the pale sea.
What holds viewers is not fish or formations —
it is the multiple columns of bubbles
rippling up from each end of the tank.

The children, particularly, key in on
the bubbles — the children whose hair is thinning
or is gone, who slowly place one foot before
the other, who find peace in their parents' arms.
The older ones wear caps and know where to go;
the parents wear masks and wait for answers.

The bubbles do not swim but swiftly rise
breaking free at the surface, gone to the light.
The children like to put their hands against
the clear glass of the tank to touch them.

––––––––

*Max Money, eighty-three, was inspired to write this poem while serving as an
American Cancer Society volunteer driver to the "Jimmy Fund" Clinic at the
Dana Farber Institute in Boston. "The children who walk the line," Money says,
"wait in innocence, hearts full of youth, chasing bubbles."*

Money has authored three books, Napa Valley Traces, Tender Threads, *and*
Worth Keeping. *He has had numerous poems published in journals — including
the* Haight-Ashbury Literary Journal, The Aurorean, *and* Red Rock Review
— and various anthologies, including The Hermit Kingdom *and* Poems of
the Korean War. *He was a contributor to* Americans' Favorite Poems *and a
Pushcart Prize nominee in 2001.*

*Money is a California native who has lived on Cape Cod since 1972. He is
a Marine Corps veteran of the Korean War and a retired public school teacher
and administrator. He is married and has three sons and five grandchildren.*

COMING BACK

by Bridget Levin

we spent her last good
day
together
playing

she was so good at playing

she wanted
a country drive
to talk about our girls going off to college

a stop for late apples and cinnamon tea

then a short hike
in the cold wind

november
was stealing in around the edges
of the afternoon

like the stomach pain she disguised
by a request to head back before dark

both of us
pretending

that neither winter

nor the cancer

was really

coming

back

Bridget Levin wrote "Coming Back" to honor a longtime friend, who died after a four-year battle from ovarian cancer. "I wrote my way through the last days of her life," she says. "Writing was all I had to hold onto as she slipped away from us. It was both a goodbye and a tribute to the beautiful life she led and the long friendship we had." She calls poetry a "portal to grief" and says, "It's an elegant way to feel and express deep sadness."

Levin's previous credits include a children's rhyming book, Rules of the Wild. *She lives in Minneapolis with her husband, their twin daughters, a frisky dog and a fat cat, aptly named Sugar Cookie.*

COMPANION

by Molly Redmond

Sorrow
slips down the chimney with the sharp night wind
seeps in the cellar through a crack in the wall
squeezes through keyholes and wrecks all your locks
bursts through the front door wrapped in the news
Sorrow
slowly infiltrates with the smell of leaves
lilts in with Mozart, keens in the strings
bangs on the windows at the middle of the day
specializes in small hours of the night
Sorrow
sneaks up behind you with a different name
catches at your throat when you watch TV
sits down beside you and shares your loaf of bread
rides in your pocket, waiting for your hand
Sorrow
drapes itself in rainbows, entices your approach
finds where you're hiding, cuts through your disguise
grabs you in your dreams and shakes you wide awake
ritually marks you with its deep-seared brand
Sorrow

---

*Molly Redmond is a nineteen-year cancer survivor and friend of many cancer
patients and survivors. She wrote this poem after the loss of a friend to breast
cancer. "It was, for their family, so very hard and long, with such cosmic shifts
in internal and external, rebalancing their lives," she says.*

Redmond had a poem in The Cancer Poetry Project, *volume one, as well.
"Poetry, by its discipline of sparseness, forces clarity and focus of thought and
language," she says. "The many emotions swirling through lives affected make
poetry's distillation all the more powerful."*

*Redmond, sixty-nine, is retired and lives near St. Paul, Minnesota, with her
husband and their "cheerful rescued golden retriever."*

EPHEMERA

by Shavawn M. Berry

Your defective breasts are gone
replaced by a fresh set, small areolas
decorating your flat, creamy chest

You smell like tortillas, corn mush;
The cremated dust of
your bones and skin belongs

to some other girl; someone
else's dismantled body
sits on a shelf at your folks' house

Brown-black hair frames your face,
a dark tide of seaweed rushing
past your neck, collarbone, shoulders

You've been dead a week
when you visit, a cherry-colored scarf
knotted at your throat

You aren't gone,
just between adventures
Abre la puerta — Open the door

You sit next to me, naked,
no more than 20 years old,
unencumbered

by the rot and shit
and bile of stage IV cancer
You hold my wrists hard

as I fight to wake,
Try to say what I —
Mi amiga, your skin is warm, salty

Everything's rustling
with scattered light
I feel your breath on my face

You speak to me in Spanish,
whole phrases float like
iridescent humingbirds

Syllables fall open,

calla lilies flush with blooms

"Mari visited me in the dream state about a week after she died," says Shavawn M. Berry, fifty-two, of her college roommate, Mari, at New York University. Mari, a theater and television actor, quit when her breast cancer metastasized. She is prominently featured in the 2011 documentary, Pink Ribbons, Inc.

"Cancer has touched my life repeatedly," says Berry, explaining why she often writes about the subject. "Besides Mari and my grandmother, my brother was diagnosed with malignant melanoma at the age of thirty-six. It is everywhere."

Berry's poetry has appeared in numerous publications, including Poet Lore, California Quarterly, *and* North Atlantic Review. *She is currently working on her first collection of poems, as well as a spiritual memoir. She is the managing editor of* Kalliope, *an online magazine.*

Berry teaches writing at Arizona State University and lives in Chandler, Arizona, with her dog, Belle, and her cats, Emma, Elvis, Ed, and Finn.

FALL APART AT THE SEAMS

by Linda DeMello

Imagine you're sitting in the emergency room
with your five-year-old daughter.
She's watching TV happily, smiling, laughing,
her entire body covered with *petechiae*
and "diffuse lymphadenopathy" of her neck.
Your husband is wearing a blank expression,
the same expression he wore at his father's funeral,
as the attending discusses whether or not
he wants to transfuse your daughter with platelets
before her bone marrow extraction in an hour.
A resident calls out from the nursing station,
her chest x-ray is back, "terrible lymphoma,"
while a medical student gawks at the film in awe.
That same medical student will visit you
frequently throughout the night,
trying to keep your neglected family company.
Everyone keeps apologizing,
"I'm sorry for this," "I'm sorry for that,"
and you just want them all to disappear.
The extraction is now postponed until tomorrow
because a trauma "rolled in,"
and they need to prioritize their operating rooms.
Delays, delays, your daughter is getting tired,
and hungry, and irritable,
and, oh God, she has cancer.
Tears are burning the back of your eyes,
bile rising in the back of your throat,
and you resist the urge to run out for a cigarette,
because you think your bad habits might've killed her.
You hate yourself in that moment,
and everyone is just so busy,
and doesn't anyone even care?

Your daughter was healthy, beautiful,
why this, why now, why her, why you?
When you finally shut the door,
closing out the bustling world,
you sit and fall apart at the seams.
When your daughter asks you,
What's wrong, mommy?
you say, Nothing, baby, nothing,
just the end of your precious life.
Your husband stares at the TV,
deadpan, stone cold,
and little do you know,
you'll be divorced in a year,
because he "can't take it anymore."

And you know what,
neither can you.

"My experience with this family stayed with me for a long time," says Linda DeMello, twenty-nine, who, as a medical student, helped care for a young patient with acute lymphoblastic leukemia and her family during an emergency room stay.

"The expression on both parents' faces when they were given their daughter's diagnosis and how the entire process ensued was just so tragic — my heart truly broke for them.... I needed to put the words down onto paper, knowing this was the only way I could possibly express what I felt, and what I believe the mom felt at the time.

She adds that it can be incredibly difficult for medical professionals, "especially newbies like me, to find the right words to say when they've never experienced the illness themselves (or any illness for that matter). Sometimes the words just hover in the air between us, and they float away when we try to catch them."

DeMello's poem, "Life's Hourglass," was published in the Journal of the American Medical Association, *in the Poetry and Medicine section, March 21, 2012. She is a fourth-year medical student at New York Medical College, planning to graduate in May 2013. She and her husband, a professional photographer, live just outside of New York City with their pets, a boxer named Kaia and two cats named Milk and Oreo.*

FOR NOEL

by Ellen Kirvin Dudis

In confirmation class we disbelieved
together, and we smirked. Myth has a way
of hanging on, of course. The other day
it came to me, and I smiled as I grieved,
you'd make one hell of an angel. But first
I like to think you turned on your disease
that withering look of humanity's
whole contempt and singularly reversed
roles, tossing some outrageous hat aside —
no wig for you. And you were good at it,
old friend, but I'm so sad. The repertoire
comes down to *ave*, hail. You went and died
without telling me you were sick, did it
all by yourself, and cancer bears the scar.

———

"*By some horrible irony, your acceptance of my poem 'For Noel,' which was written
a couple of years ago, arrived the same day as the news that my own liver cancer
was no longer treatable and my chemo program was ended,*" wrote Ellen Kirvin
Dudis, seventy, on July 19, 2012. "*Nevertheless, I'm happy that my thoughts
about an old friend's struggle with this terrible disease would be passed along
to the many who have suffered as patients or as caregivers like my own dear
husband.*" Dudis passed away less than two weeks later.

After pursuing a career in advertising, Dudis, a native New Yorker, and her
husband, Joseph Dudis, started an evergreen nursery, Five Deer Farm, near
Pocomoke City, Maryland. Her poems have appeared in numerous anthologies
and journals. She was also a busy volunteer and loved gardening, cutting firewood,
fishing, and exploring the deserted barrier islands of Virginia's Eastern Shore.

She was survived by her husband; her son, Daniel; her daughter, Susan; her
sister, Chloe; and, according to her obituary, "by hundreds, if not thousands, of
white pines, blue spruce, Leyland cypress, magnolias, Douglas firs, Norway
spruce, and Atlas cedars transported by customers to the four corners of Delmarva.
One particularly stunning white pine, first planted in 1975, now towers more
than fifty feet above her beloved farm."

A FRIEND'S PRAYER FOR YOU

by Linda Jett

I wish I had the power to bathe you in an ocean of peace,
to offer you the soothing sounds of constant tides,
to place your feet upon the sand with its tiny grains,
shaped by the adversities of many storms, shifting yet solid.

I wish I had the power to immerse you in reassurance;
but I am not God.

Instead I offer paltry prayers for you,
trusting the Spirit to open them
before the One who is our Beginning and our End.
The Creator of the oceans listens to our hearts' cries
above the sounds of life.

For today that is enough.

Linda Jett, sixty-four, wrote this poem for Robin, a friend and a client, who endured three types of cancer. "Throughout this entire saga, she never lost her gentle sense of humor or her faith," says Jett. "As a testament to her positive attitude, the hospital staff often chose to spend their free time visiting with her in her room. Many came to her memorial service to give witness to her positive impact on their lives." Jett says she "longed to help carry her burden so I'd periodically send her cards and poems."

Jett has contributed to inspirational short story collections and devotional books. Her poetry often appears in newsletters, especially those of Oregon Christian Writers of which she is a member.

Jett has been a teacher, a children's librarian, and, for the past thirty-five years, a massage therapist. She and her husband both love to read so she is currently dedicated to hooking all three of their grandchildren on the joys of reading. She lives in Newberg, Oregon.

HARBINGER

by Perie Longo

When the owl returned last night,
I should have rushed down the street
and held you, held you together
knowing full well the speed of fall
when a lifelong mate takes flight.

In the dark, for the longest time
I watched it walk the high wire
between your house and mine, back and forth,

like the Frenchman Philippe Petite, whose passion
was making art out of his body and air.

Long before the Twin Towers came crashing down,

he danced between them on a wire in high winds and fog.

Mirage of bird, crowds far below
must have thought in their rush to work.
And staring up in disbelief, stopped.
Once descended, reporters asked him why.

"To humanize them," he said,
        "make visible the edge between life and death."

The morning after the owl's visit, racing to work,
I finally understood your presence in the driveway, staring
at the sky, bereft. Your wife was gone. I yanked
on the emergency brake, left
the engine running, leapt out, held you then in the wind.

In certain light

    she'll seem not
    far away.

Perie Longo, seventy-one, wrote this poem for a friend. "I saw Ronald standing in his driveway, talking on his cell phone and looking up at the sky, and I knew his wife, Rachel, my friend, had died." Longo says she understood Ronald's situation, because her husband had died ten years before of chronic lymphocitic leukemia.

Longo has three books of poetry: Milking the Earth, The Privacy of Wind, *and* With Nothing Behind But Sky. *Her poems have appeared in numerous journals, including* Nimrod, Paterson Literary Review, *and* Prairie Schooner.

Longo is Poet Laureate Emerita of Santa Barbara, California (2007-09). She is a psychotherapist, a registered poetry therapist, past president of The National Association for Poetry Therapy, and, for twenty-five years, both a teacher with California Poets in the Schools and a member of the literary staff of Santa Barbara Writers' Conference. She has two children, Dana and Cecily, and three grandchildren, India, Paloma, and Zane.

HIRED MAN DOWN

by Maryann (Wendy) Hurtt

the hired man
lies in musty sheets and patched quilts
his room partitioned
from the barn
stacks of *National Geographic*
piled neatly in the corner
dry hay, greasy tools,
and manure insulate
against early spring chill

his one window
leaks the farm kids' giggles
they tiptoe into his room
rock back and forth
with questions
about the old man they never knew
to be down

his breaths get noisy
his gut is draining away
the air around him
fills with odor
so different than the sweet smell of manure

he knows what he has to do
lie low, breathe in, breathe out
slower and slower

the animals taught him well
this is, after all, no tragedy
but what we must all do someday
this man just more intimate
with the cycles
the rest of us still fear

Maryann (Wendy) Hurtt, sixty-three, served as a hospice nurse for the patient in this poem. "He had been the hired man on a farm for many years," she says. "He really did live in the barn, and the family he worked for cared for him there. Out his one window, I could hear the kids, see early spring crops starting to make their rows, smell the manure. I kept thinking about how animals lie low when they are dying. He really understood life without reading self-help books.

"Poetry and cancer get to the essence of life quickly and succinctly. When I work as a hospice nurse, I want to know what is really important to that person; when I write, I want to convey that respect and to take deep notice of what is happening." Her publishing credits include Wisconsin People and Ideas, FreeVerse, Echos, *and* Stoneboat.

Hurtt is a registered nurse, rides a bright yellow tandem bicycle with her husband, and is starting to write, communicate and sometimes dream in Czech having recently studied at Charles University in Prague.

LANDFALL

by Ann Cefola

The bruised body falls back into its water weight. Into the green-cold
your husband jumps, pushing the abandoned man onto his boat's lower grill.
Lips against a swollen mouth, your husband blows then yells,
C'mon, goddammit. Come back.

You know where the man is. Fingering grit and rusted can,
slapping starfish and seaweed aside, you call your own blue body,
sinking from slices and stitches as unfamiliar as fin and scale.
Can you coax yourself back from a diagnosis's murky deep?

On land, stunned rescuers savor the give of grass, foam and spike of air.
Like fish on newsprint, gills fanning, the saved man lays stretcher-soft,
breath regular as the red strobe above him. You too rise pink, lungs hard,
ravenous for salt scent, bold spinnakers, a mooring's late night knocks.

This silver net of chance, sky and water meeting,
winds together your husband, the fisherman and your new formed self.
Healing feels like work, like running up the biggest sail.

---

*Ann Cefola, fifty-five, wrote this poem for a friend and has another, "Breast
Imaging," on page 12. "Poetry is about the hard as well as the joyful journeys,"
she says. "Before we had electronic media, people turned to literature to learn
how to live. Poetry especially tells us not only how to survive but how to thrive
in the face of enormous personal challenge. In a compact space, between lyrical
images, something escapes that feels a little divine."*

Cefola's previously published works have appeared in Sugaring, St. Agnes,
Pink-Slipped, *and the translation* Hence this cradle.

*Cefola works as a communications professional. As for her hobbies, she says,
"I am crazy in love with pit bull-type dogs and, in my spare time, advocate for
desperately needed shelter reform in New York City."*

LEAVING THE CLINIC
— Baja California, 2011

by Marilyn Taylor

Having carried your own
terrible frailness
to the edge of the water

you bent your body sharply
like a broken stick, until
you were kneeling in the sand.

If the world weren't so damned
beautiful, you said, maybe
dying wouldn't be so bad —

But then you saw how a small rain
had pocked the creamy skin
of the beach overnight

causing snails to leave their sanctuaries,
and the pursed hibiscus buds
to fatten and explode,

and with the sea collapsing around us,
thinning to a glassy sheen
that blinded you

you hid your face
behind your hands and shook
with unrequited love.

Marilyn L. Taylor wrote this poem for a friend and poetry student who succumbed to cervical cancer. "She showed enormous courage throughout, and I felt compelled to try to write a poem in her honor," says Taylor, who also lost her husband to cancer in 2012.

Taylor, former poet laureate of Wisconsin (2009 and 2010) and Milwaukee (2004 and 2005), is author of six poetry collections. Her poems and essays have appeared in many anthologies and journals, including Poetry, The American Scholar, *and* Able Muse, *plus Ted Kooser's "American Life in Poetry" column.*

Taylor taught poetry and poetics for fifteen years at the University of Wisconsin-Milwaukee, and serves on the advisory board of the MFA Program in creative writing at Western State College, Gunnison, Colorado. She is also a contributing editor for The Writer *magazine.*

Taylor has a son and a daughter-in-law; is active in a "wonderfully warm and welcoming" poetry community in Madison, Wisconsin; and lives with a goldendoodle and two nondescript but intellectually gifted cats.

LIFE ACCORDING TO SADIE

by Kim M. Baker

So what are you in for?
You would think pink would hide
blood stains, now wouldn't you.
Ovarian. Woulda preferred breast.
Just lop 'em off like Bobbit!
None a this abdominal surgery.
Like slicin' open a cat in grammar school.
Or was that high school? Chemo brain.
No, no, my last treatment.
They give me six months to two years.
Like a prison sentence. Short prison sentence.
Oh, no, Honey, don't feel bad.
At least I won't have to wear any more of these blasted hats.
Hand me that newspaper, would ya?
Can you believe this new governor?
Imagine taxin' my eyeglasses and my coffin.
My sister got a good laugh about that one.
She wears glasses too.
Over there on her Crackberry, talking to her hubby,
who's waiting for her patiently on the San Diego golf course.
My sister Grace. I call her my chemo wife, though.
Connubial by cancer.
No, my man retired and then dropped dead from boredom.
Never did even one thing on his honey-do list.
Yeah, my Gracie came in December when I started my first round.
She's been here so long, we finishing each other's sentences now.
Sure wish we could finish each other's lives.

Hey, Cheryl! That's Cheryl from the American Cancer Society.
Hey, Cheryl! You got any of those little pink pillows?
Get Betsy here one, will ya? Her feets are hurtin' her at night.
During chemo, sheets feel like damned concrete. You like pink, Honey?
Funny. I never thought of cancer as pink.
Always thought of it more like a rancid can of sardines.
You take care too, Honey. And don't worry none.
Boobs ain't nothin' but pink pillows.
Better under your head. Or your feet.

After her partner was diagnosed with breast cancer, Kim M. Baker, fifty-six, often accompanied her to "Camp Chemo." Today, she is in remission.

"So many people there look frightened and depressed, for good reason," Baker says. "I met one woman who had only a little while longer to live, but she was upbeat and always trying to reach out to and comfort the other patients. I was so moved, I had to write about her kick-ass attitude." In fact, Baker turned this poem into a dramatic monologue, which has been read at the Culture Park Annual Short Play Marathon in New Bedford, Massachusetts.

Baker's poems have been published online and in print; her essays have been broadcast on This I Believe *and NPR Rhode Island; and another of her plays has been stage read as well.*

When Baker is not "teaching the abundant virtues of the comma at Roger Williams University School of Law, writing poetry about big hair and Elvis, or doing the cha-cha," she is working to end violence against women. She makes her home in Rhode Island with her minister partner and a diva cat.

The Cancer Poetry Project 2

LIKE SMOKE

by Jim Pahz

Where do Marlboro men go to die?

When they dismount,
which comes off first,
the saddle or the
oxygen tank?

Is there a Boot Hill for smokers?

> "Yonder lies Philip Morris…
> Over there, Sir Walter Raleigh."

They said there was "always something happening
at Joe's place."

Not anymore.

The camel's gone,
almost forgotten.

I can't even remember…

Did he have
one hump

or two?

Jim Pahz's father-in-law was a lifelong cigarette smoker who didn't believe the health warnings about smoking until it was too late. "He, like many in his generation," says Pahz, sixty-nine, "was taken in by cigarette advertising propaganda and smoked Camels until he died." He died six months after a diagnosis of lung cancer.

"When cancer touches someone we love, it has a profound influence," he says, "not just on the patient, but on all the family members as well. Poetry is a way to sort through feelings and gain perspective."

Pahz has four chapbooks: Saving Turtles, Almost Chosen… Nearly Saved, McAngel, *and* Finding Quetzal. *He lives with his wife, Cheryl, in central Michigan.*

NIGHT AT THE OPERA

by Marc Straus

Blood gushing, severed limbs flying everwhere.
I am laughing uncontrollably. It's *Chain Saw Massacre
Number IV,* and Lisa is yelling from under the
pillow, *Dad, you're a big sicko.* My son, Jason,

won't ever watch a horror film with me. I had mocked
Alien. I couldn't help it. The goop dribbling
from the monster's mouth was hilarious. It's too late
for my wife to complain. After our first date (we saw

Psycho at the Rialto), she said that Norman Bates
was a modern Oedipus tragedy, and I said that Norman
was the funniest character I had seen in a movie
since the great Groucho in *Night at the Opera.*

Doesn't anything ever scare you, Daddy? Lisa
recently asked me. Yes, I said. I am frightened
out of my mind each time I see Glioblastoma multiforme,
and for every kid with acute lymphocytic leukemia.

---

*Marc Straus is a mostly retired oncologist who has opened a contemporary art
gallery, Marc Straus LLC, on New York's Lower Eastside. He has three collections
of poetry from TriQuarterly Books, Northwestern University Press.* Not God, *the
most recent book, is a play in verse that has been staged Off Broadway. The two
characters are a woman hospitalized with cancer and her oncologist; various
poems have since been added to the play, including the poem here.*

    *Straus is the recipient of numerous poetry awards, including a residency
at Yaddo and the Robert Penn Warren Award in the Humanities from Yale
Medical School. His poems have appeared in many leading journals. He lives
with his wife, Livia, whom he met on the first day of ninth grade. They have
two children and five grandchildren.*

NOTHING TO WORRY ABOUT

by Bobbi Hahn

It's just a small bump, really,
nothing
to be concerned about.
I found it this morning
in the shower, during
the Monthly Breast Self-Exam
my gynecologist is always
harping about.
I finally began checking myself
just to shut her up.
At first,
I honestly didn't even
notice it.
It's so small,
it can't even
really be called
a lump.
I was initially upset
but since it's so tiny —
really insignificant
actually —
I'll just wait until
next month's
self-exam
to see if it's
still there.

"The experiences of my friends and my own reluctance to perform a monthly self-exam prompted this piece," says Bobbi Hahn, seventy. "I imagine that many women are similarly recalcitrant, although we've all heard the warnings about how vital it is." She wrote this to honor several friends who have had breast cancer; all are survivors. "Sadly, though, I've lost three friends and my precious 'daughter-in-love' to brain cancer."

Hahn has published magazine features, essays and poems, and has four still-in-progress books. Over the years, she has worked at several jobs, including travel agent, community theater manager, needlework shop owner, and art gallery manager.

Hahn lives with John, her husband of forty-seven years, and cat, Mozart, on Hilton Head Island, South Carolina. They wish they could see their three grown sons, grandchildren, and great-grandchildren more often.

ONLY LIFE

by Don Colburn

It's only life, my friend would say
when everydayness leaned in
on him. I knew not to take him lightly,
for Vic was older and had been to war,
had lost a job or two, a wife,
his shirt in the market.
Plus, Vic is from Minneapolis
and rarely overstates things. Not bad, he said,
when Jack Morris pitched 10 shutout innings
in the seventh game of the World Series
or spring showed up with daffodils
after a week of cold rain.
For years, I knew exactly what
Vic was saying about his life
and mine: no biggie, suck it up, don't think
so much about your own stubbed toe.
Until today, when we met for lunch
at the Chinese place in Vic's high-rise
so he wouldn't have to walk outside.
First time I'd seen him since the biopsy
and the start of what's left.
Vic was wearing an old Twins ballcap,
not wanting to scare me. We hugged
clumsily and sat. *You know what Adam said
to Eve in the Garden,* he deadpanned,
and I laughed at his punch line, same
as in the old days. We ordered egg rolls,
asparagus and sweet-and-sour shrimp,
with chopsticks and tea. Like before.

Then, mid-sentence, Vic's voice
gave out and he held up one hand
to say, *don't worry, this won't be pretty*
but give me a moment — and coughed
from way down, a slurry ruckus.
He gathered himself to finish
his thought, then caught a breath.
It's only life, I blurted,
hating what I had just said,
except Vic raised his index finger
and smiled and nodded: But life.

Don Colburn, sixty-five, is a writer in Portland, Oregon. During a long career
as a health reporter for newspapers, including The Washington Post *and*
The Oregonian, *he interviewed hundreds of people touched by cancer. Among*
the many fine journalists he worked with at The Washington Post *was Victor*
Cohn, once known as the dean of American newspaper science and medical
writers. Colburn says Cohn helped his colleagues keep things in perspective
with wry humor, exemplified by his oft-repeated remark: "It's only life."

"Like many of Vic's aphorisms, this one got more complicated — and wiser
— the more you thought about it," says Colburn. "And it became all the
more poignant when Vic, during a busy retirement, fell ill with lung cancer."
"Only Life" appeared first in Cider Press Review.

Colburn has published one book of poems, As If Gravity Were a Theory,
and two chapbooks: Another Way to Begin *and* Because You Might Not
Remember. *His many writing honors include the Discovery/The Nation Award,*
the Finishing Line Prize and the Cider Press Book Award. He was a finalist
for the Pulitzer Prize in feature writing. His latest manuscript is a sequence of
poetic monologues called Tomorrow Too: The Brenda Monologues, *based on*
the true story of a woman facing breast cancer and pregnancy at the same time.

ON THE THIRD FLOOR AT
MOSES CONE MEMORIAL HOSPITAL

by Steve Cushman

Pushing the portable x-ray machine
on my way to do a STAT chest on a Mr. Wilson
in 3002, I spotted two old ladies standing
in the hall, leaning against their IV poles.
They both had to be in their 70s, decked out
in loose hospital gowns, red skid-proof socks
stuffed into white slippers from home.

They were laughing as if this was where they
wanted to spend a Tuesday afternoon.
One of the ladies had white hair and the other red.
I didn't realize the red hair was a wig
until the white-haired lady reached up to straighten it,
as if to say, *come on, let's get ourselves together*
here. And the lady with the wig blushed
as if to say, *aren't we beyond all that now?*
And the other lady shook her head
as if to say, *no, we never really are.*

Like the poem's narrator, Steve Cushman, forty-four, is an x-ray technologist.
"This poem was written in the spirit of that patient who tries to do the best she
can with what has happened to her," he says. "For many years, I primarily
wrote fiction. I avoided writing about patients or hospital situations, but as
I've recently turned to poetry, so many of the images of patients and medical
situations I've accumulated over the years have come out as I try and chronicle
some of what I've seen."

Cushman has two published novels, Portisville *and* Heart with Joy, *as well*
as a short-story collection, Fracture City. *His first poetry chapbook,* Hospital
Work, *is due out in 2013.*

Cushman received his Master of Fine Arts in fiction writing from the
University of North Carolina at Greensboro. He and his wife, who also works
in radiology, have a ten-year-old son. They live in Greensboro.

ON THIS NIGHT

by M.S. Rooney

of rain falling,
ditches overflowing,
fields flooding,
the car loses water
and the heat needle
moves up, up,
but does not quite hit
the bright red zone,
and so I drive on to meet you.

How can you bear
what you have heard today,
your own death so close?

I do not know what we say,
know only the yielding
to that place
where words do not intrude
on meaning.

Later, we fill the radiator,
find a mechanic to patch it up
enough so I can drive
the twenty miles home.

On the road,
the needle rests
between red and blue,
as if all is well,
as if all is well,
as if I can drive through
this night.

M.S. Rooney's friend of almost twenty years, Janette Buchman, died of thyroid cancer at age fifty-two. "Janette met the disease with every resource she could find, yet when she knew her death was near, rather than sinking into fear or bitterness, she embraced and savored every moment she had left," says Rooney.

Buchman not only planned her memorial, but wrote a piece to be read to her family and friends. It ends with this: "I believe that we are on a spiritual continuum, that we have been together, we are together, and we will continue to be together — in love and spirit. The connection I have felt particularly over these past few months has been phenomenal. The power and flow of energy has been buoying and strengthening.... I thank you, and I thank the power of the universe for this incredible gift, creating the best season of my life. It has been my great good fortune to have experienced unconditional love. May you feel it now."

Rooney lives in Sonoma, California, with her husband, poet Dan Noreen. Her work has appeared in journals and anthologies, including Bluestem, The Cortland Review, *and* The Main Street Rag.

PETER RABBIT

by Carol Burcham Grommesh

I'm running for Pete, because she couldn't be here today.

Pete was tall, dark, and had Diana Ross hair.
She was beautiful and graceful, and none of what her name implied.
Before her hair fell out, she bought a wig, so that we didn't quite know when
the mane stopped being hers.

The last day she was in the office, we didn't know how to say goodbye,
so we planned her wedding instead.
She was going to get married on Valentine's Day to Scottie Pippen.
But on Valentine's Day, Pete was too busy dying to be a bride, and Scottie
was too busy winning another ring to hand one to a woman he'd never met.

I didn't know Pete's real name until her funeral.
I don't remember it now, except that it started with "A" and didn't fit her.
I wore a mint green dress to the funeral, because Pete was too joyful to
remember in black, and besides, it was the dress I would have worn to the wedding.

Her family called her "Peter Rabbit" as a child; she loved the story of the
little bunny who cheated death.
She fought, too, and cheated death for a while.
Peter shed his coat, struggling to get through the hole in the fence.

Pete shed her breast, then her hair, and finally her whole body.
So now I'm running with thousands of other people all in the same T-shirts.
And Pete's name is carefully lettered on the pink sign on my back.

I'm running for Pete, because she couldn't be here today.

Carol Burcham Grommesh, forty-seven, was inspired to write this poem by the loss of a coworker to breast cancer.

"I've written poetry about other things," she says, "but this poem was born of a combination of an interesting story, the Dallas Race for the Cure (run by a nonrunner), and the experience of having read The Cancer Poetry Project, *volume one. I kept thinking as I was running that what I was enduring was nothing compared to what people fighting cancer endure."*

Grommesh formerly worked in retail as a buyer and business analyst. Her son, Daniel, "introduced me to the world of special education" with his speech delay and later diagnosis of autism. She now works as a teacher of elementary-aged students with significant cognitive and physical disabilities. A South Dakota native, Grommesh lives with her husband and two children in Lewisville, Texas.

PICKING UP RONNA FOR PHYSICAL THERAPY AT THE CHAMPA STREET GYM

by Madelyn Garner

We find her fallen   hairless head turned toward us   arms folded over
wounded chest   throbbing in skin soft as yolk   bones shell fragile   and
we   full like ticks of excellent blood   lift her safely back into her nest
of rumpled sheets and pillows.   Still, she insists,   please carry me   and we do
from home to car and over the gym's pasturage of mats.   Now as gray skies
stream through city-stained glass   she lifts weights hardly heavier than twigs.
Frail warrior bench-perched and unbending.   Who minds the arms that bob and
weave?   Or the heart?   It's thinning blood   and yet it pumps.   Ronna rises.
Waving us away   laughs at our applause.

"*Ronna died from breast cancer after almost a decade of trying various treatments
— surgical, chemical, and biological,*" *says Madelyn Garner, seventy-five. To
repay various kindnesses, Ronna* "*would bring unexpected treats, usually a latte
and a sweet roll in my case. I will never forget looking up from my desk to find
her balancing a sack and coffee cup even though she needed a walker to get from
her car to the school office.*"

*Garner is the recipient of writing fellowships and prizes, including the
Aspen Writers' Conference Fellowship, the D.H. Lawrence Award from the
University of New Mexico, and the Jackson Hole Writers Conference Poetry
Prize. Recent work has appeared in* Nimrod International Journal, American
Journal of Nursing, *and the anthology* Beyond Forgetting, Poetry and Prose
about Alzheimer's Disease, *among others. She is co-editor of* Collecting Life:
Poets on Objects Known and Imagined.

*Garner, recently retired again from a position in education, currently works
in Denver as an editor, publisher, and freelance writer. Her two daughters and
three grandchildren live nearby so she is able to enjoy them on a daily basis.
Her son, Bradley, died in 1996.*

PLAYING IN THE BAND

by Richard M. Berlin

All over this moonlit mountain, neighbors call
the cops, and the cops call, *Turn it down!*
but it's too late to stop "Wild Night"
with a hundred people dancing so hard
they've thrown off their shoes.
I'm turning fifty with a starburst
guitar hanging on my hips,
rhythm hand keyed to the high hat cymbal,
and when Billy rakes E-D-A and sings,
Let me tell you 'bout my baby,
we crank it up another notch,
sweat pouring, wine pouring,
fireflies flashing like a marquee,
Billy belting out *G-L-O-R-I-A, Gloria!*
his hair grown back from chemo, a glory,
my stepfather, on vacation from chemo, a glory,
Steven, smiling, one day post-chemo, a glory,
James in his tux, finished with chemo, a glory,
Marlena and my mother dancing
without their breasts, a glory,
all of us shimmering in summer's halo,
bandaged by rags of music and moonlight,
playing in this glorious band of the living,
shaking in time to our lives.

When Richard M. Berlin, M.D., sixty-two, began to write this poem about his fiftieth birthday party, he thought he was going to write about the police coming to shut down the loud music. "But as I wrote," he says, "my focus turned to our lead guitarist who had just finished chemotherapy for lymphoma. Then I realized just how many people at the party had survived cancer, and that is where the poem took me."

Berlin practices psychiatry in the Berkshire Hills of western Massachusetts. He has published two poetry chapbooks and is the author of two book-length collections of poems. How JFK Killed My Father *won the 2002 Pearl Poetry Prize.* Secret Wounds *won the John Ciardi Award in Poetry from BkMk Press, was a finalist for the ForeWord Book Prize, and won the USA Book News Award as the best general poetry book published in 2011. "Playing in the Band" is part of that collection.*

Berlin is also editor of Poets on Prozac: Mental Illness, Treatment, and the Creative Process. *His poems, which focus on life as a physician, have appeared in his monthly column in* Psychiatric Times *for the past twelve years. Berlin is married to Susanne L. King, M.D., a child/adolescent psychiatrist and health-care reform activist. Their daughter, Rachel, is a third-year medical student at the University of Massachusetts Medical School.*

THE POISON WOMB

by Christina McDaniel

The child was made in spring
    when the heather was breaking

through the valley,
    before the tumors broke the heart.

Mother and father
    walk hand in hand from

oncology to maternity.
    Her pink hospital gown

covers her belly, a bell
    jar she wishes to fill with

birds of paradise
    and hope and other pretty

things. He is
    their first born. They will

call him Jonah.
    With quivering fingers,

she unties
    her bandana and bows

her head, her long hair
    striped with bald patches.

She crumples the silk
    in her hand, touches her heart.

Noticing her tears,
     her husband guides her hand

onto her belly.
     She cannot feel her child kicking.

She fears the poison
     seeped underneath the bell jar,

dissolving her son
     into pieces. She crumbled,

could not breathe,
     twisted her bandana

in knots,
     sobbed, *Where is he?*

He lives in
     the snows of next January

in the arms of
     a woman in a red cap,

her hair returning
     beneath it like the heather

under the snow. She is
     not yet made or born

of the needles
     and the machines, watching her

husband shovel away
     the consequences of the blizzard.

Jonah is
    a little survivor fish,

with round knees
    and ten fingers.

His heartbeat holds the room.
    Something is starting to happen.

"I wrote this poem on behalf of young mothers who refuse to compromise their hopes of raising a family to accommodate their disease," says Christina McDaniel, twenty-one. "More precisely, this poem is a tribute to my best friend's mother who was diagnosed with breast cancer when my friend was a couple of months old. My friend laughs, remembering stories of how as an infant, she would reach up and pull off her mother's wig."

McDaniel also wrote the poem to honor her sister-in-law, who was diagnosed with thyroid cancer just a couple of months after her only daughter's first birthday. "I watched her go through the fear of potentially having to spend several days away from her daughter in isolation while the oncologists treated her with oral radiation." She has since given birth to another child, a healthy baby boy.

McDaniel has had fiction and poetry published in Polaris Literary Magazine, Ruminate Magazine, *and* The Soundings Review. *She is a student at Oakland University in Detroit, Michigan, working toward her bachelor's degree in English and creative writing. She lives with her father, a cancer survivor, and five cats.*

PRAYER SHAWL

by Mimi Moriarty

The intravenous pinches, you wince
we chat the hours into manageable bits
I drive you home, prayer shawl
encircling your shoulders

an elderly nun knit your shawl
with every stitch she concealed
a prayer, a holy recitation
to brace you

the warm breath of the old nun
huffs away affliction
as if it were cobwebs
and you were a standing barn

the prayers take hold
the reversal takes hold
the reckless cancer
releases its hold

but you remain shaven
for now, awaiting the
return of your hair
and hope

you carefully coordinate
your headscarf to your shawl,
its own beauty fragile as ash,
reflecting

the movement of needle
over needle, prayer
over healing
prayer.

Mimi Moriarty, sixty-eight, wrote this poem to honor her friend, Maureen Moran, who lived for five years with ovarian cancer. "During those five years," she says. *"Maureen was very active in the Teal Run and raised thousands of dollars. Her family and friends continue to support the Teal Run in her memory."*

Moriarty has three chapbooks: War Psalm, Sibling Reverie *(co-written with her brother, Frank R. Desiderio, CSP), and* Crows Calling.

Moriarty lives in a log home overlooking Albany, New York, with her husband, Dan. She considers it her retirement home, even though Dan still works. They raised three children and have four grandchildren living nearby.

Moriarty has zigzagged her way through life, enjoying every job she has held, from catering to family life ministry. Her interest in poetry emerged several years ago, prompting her to return to school. She earned a Master of Fine Arts degree from Goddard College in 2004.

RONALD MCDONALD HOUSE

by Tony Gloeggler

My friend Dave said
it's a great place to meet
women and I wanted
to start a writing group
for the kids with cancer,
their brothers and sisters.
But half the kids barely
speak English and the women
all sell advertising space
or work on Wall Street.
We sit around a table
as long as the Last Supper,
gesture, smile and repeat
polite phrases while making
collages. The women stay
in groups of two or three
like sixth grade and talk
about Upper East Side
rents, Mariah Carey
and parties on Fire Island.
No one wonders out loud
about the missing kids;
if Nicky's down the block
eating pizza with his twin
sister visiting from Greece,
whether Aaron went home
to die in Las Vegas, Nevada.
I keep my head down, busy
filling construction paper
with armies of stick figures
and stenciled letters that spell
out the names of dead guitar
players and old girlfriends

until a kid calls my name,
wants to play ping-pong.

Tonight, I'm playing ball
with Anthony. He's five,
maybe six, can't catch for shit
and since his hair fell out
he looks like the leader
of the Smashing Pumpkins.
His round, beaming face
bobs up and down
to the bouncing ball
like a cartoon sing-along
and I find myself singing silly
summer songs. You want
to hear that Anthony short
hops a grounder and flips it
underhand like Knoblauch
starting an inning-ending
double play. You want me
to say he traps the ball
in his lap, waves it over
his head like he's caught
a Mark McGwire home run.
But no, really, he kind of claps
his hands together and the ball
pops up, bounces across
the table, knocking down a castle
of blocks, and this little girl,
this dark-haired pretty little girl,
starts crying and nothing
the women volunteers, me
or even her mother tries
helps at all. She keeps
crying, louder and deeper,
and I swear I'd bang her head
on the floor, if I thought
it could make her stop.

"My poem is all about my experience volunteering for Ronald McDonald House," says Tony Gloeggler. *"I saw that the kids enjoyed hanging out and doing stuff with me and the other volunteers as a recess from what they were going through, but I mostly felt frustrated at not being able to do more, be more help. I was a lot younger then and since my real job was and is running group homes for developmentally disabled folks, I sort of missed being able to have more of a part in their lives. I only volunteered for half a year and the experience kept eating at me, the frustration of not being involved enough, not being able to unrealistically make things 'all better.'"*

Gloeggler's poems have been in numerous journals. His full-length collection, One Wish Left *(Pavement Saw Press, 2000), went into a second edition. His other collections are* Tony Gloeggler's Greatest Hits *(Pudding House Publications, 2009) and* The Last Lie *(NYQ Books, 2010). Gloeggler lives in New York City.*

THE SUMMER SOLSTICE

by John Manesis

You showed me the mammogram
and pointed to a white star
in the dark sky of my breast —
how innocent and far away it seemed,
a sparkle on the horizon,
but I could tell that you, stargazer,
had seen that heavenly sign many times.
When you excised the cancer,
no bigger than a fingertip,
I saw the red glare of my incision,
a half moon reflected in your glasses.
No need to remove your breast, you said —
had you done so, how could I have filled
the emptiness, the darkness of space?
Heal my wound the way Heracles
had his charioteer, Iolaus,
seal the gashes of Hydra.
I need your magic,
not your strength.

———————

*"The patient described in 'The Summer Solstice' is a composite of many breast
cancer patients, who have been shown their mammograms and required
biopsies,"* says John Manesis, M.D., seventy-six. *A retired radiologist, he had
interpreted myriad mammograms and, before that, as a clinician, discussed cases
with cancer patients.*

*"Poetry helps a physician understand the emotional and physical impact
cancer has on patients by asking relevant questions: How will the biopsy affect
this woman? Will it alter her self-image? Will she be able to deal with a possible
mastectomy? How does she put her trust in the surgeon?"*

*Manesis' poetry has appeared in seventy-five literary publications. His
published poetry books include* With All My Breath, Other Candle Lights,
Consider, If You Will *and, his latest,* In the Third Season. *He lives in Palm
Desert, California.*

SWEETIE, SWEETIE

by Margot Wizansky

Dead, you aren't pretty,
naked, ruined beneath the quilt,
skin like laundry on a drying rack.

Your eyes won't close,
your cheeks concave,
I can't talk about your breasts.
Your belly's slumped
but your feet are alabaster,
beautiful and strange,
each toe a little plumped-up pillow.

Each of us greets you —
dry, warm, unresisting,
thin as a parachute,
downed and settling slowly.
We dampen napkins
in a basin, stroke your arms, legs,
rub your chest.

We pour tiny pools of oil
into each other's palms
and crooning to you,
shine your body.

Part by part, we shroud you,
bodice, bib for your throat, tunic,
all ravel-edged, homespun, square,
tie the headpiece under your chin,
cloak your swollen white hands in a sack,
pull on the trousers, the bottoms sewn shut,
one, two three, together lift
the heavy sum of weightlessness.

Oh, Sweetie, sweetie,
we are your five friends, trembling,
the closest we've ever been to you
and you aren't here.

---

*"'Sweetie, sweetie' five of us crooned to our friend as we washed her body and
shrouded her for burial," says Margot Wizansky, seventy-one, of her friend who
died from ovarian cancer. "Our dying friend had asked us to do this for her.
We'd been called to her deathbed at midnight. I began to write in the early
morning hours when I couldn't sleep away the images of that singular and
profound experience. It was uplifting because we had been able to give our
friend some comfort, and it was heartbreaking, as well."*

"Sweetie, Sweetie" has been previously published four times, in the
Antigonish Review, Kalliope, The Ibbetson Review, *and in The Boston
Herald Community Poetry Contest.*

*Wizansky lives with her husband, David, in Massachusetts. He calls himself
her "poetry dog," following at her heels, holding stacks of books, her coffee cup,
and her umbrella while she waits in line at book signings. They have two grown
children, both artists who live on the West Coast.*

*Wizansky still works in the business she and her husband founded thirty
years ago, creating housing for adults with intellectual challenges. In her spare
time, she is a poet and a painter, most recently of pet portraits — dogs, horses,
chickens, and cows.*

THE TRAIN

by Elizabeth Winthrop

I am not there at the end. None of the friends are.
You lie in the fairyland bed your children made for you
in the living room. Someone brings over the chrysalis
of a monarch butterfly, a pale green sac
glued to a bare branch but you do not live to see it bloom
into an orange-and-black-winged flower
headed some day soon for Mexico. The children play music for you
and when you open your eyes, you can see
the hearth your husband built in the house
years ago before he died himself
like you; too young, too early.

They say at the end you begin to stir and become agitated
as if you are holding back, reluctant to get on the train
that is waiting in the station. But the children gather around
stroke your withered limbs, the wrinkled skin sliding off
your bald skull. They love you into death,
whisper to you about who has gone before
who is waiting around the corner in the next compartment.
They tell you it is time to get on the train,
let it carry you away, nothing to be scared of anymore,
no more battles, needles, chemicals.
You must hear them because you stop thrashing,
you breathe once, twice a long time later
and then no third time.

I am in Virginia when I hear
the news three hours after you die
on a warm October evening.
It still feels like summer here.
Two bluebirds dance around their box
perched on the fence outside my studio.
The crickets are busy in the fields.

I am surrounded by strangers
and I tell a blonde artist in a black pantsuit
what has happened. Her eyes narrow in sympathy, she tilts
her head, recommends a sleeping pill.
But I have no trouble falling asleep.
Tears have always tired me out.
I wake at four-thirty in the morning
to the sudden rush and rattle of a freight train,
very near, a wall of noise that comes on loud
and then takes itself away again.
I imagine that is your goodbye to me,
your spirit stopping in to blow me a kiss
as it whistles its way on up the line.

Elizabeth Winthrop (a.k.a. Elizabeth Winthrop Alsop), sixty-four, wrote poems during her friend's breast cancer as a way of holding on to her while at the same time, learning to let her go. "The Train" captures best "that moment when I understood that she was on her own journey and I could only accompany her part of the way."

Winthrop is a memoirist and a writer of fiction for all ages. Her most recent publications include Maia and the Monster Baby, *a picture book for young children, and* Don't Knock Unless You're Bleeding, *a memoir about growing up in Washington, D.C., in the 1950s as the daughter of journalist Stewart Alsop. Winthrop, the mother of two children and the grandmother of twin girls, divides her time between New York City and the Berkshires.*

TRAINSPOTTING IN THE CLINIC

by Majid Mohiuddin

We talked about his trains:
HO and N gauge, and even Z,
which is two-hundred-twenty times smaller
than the real Santa Fe he rode as a kid
and is now too small to paint in his withered, shaking hands
that swell on a sunny morning before
the next day of surprise showers.

We talked about the majestic mountains:
he carved them out of stacked, blue Styrofoam blocks,
then melted edges with hot wires to fall in butter avalanches
and covered them with plaster cheesecloth
and brushed hues of brown, grey, and green,
and glued sprinkled gravel and grass into
undulating meadows at the base
with a blue trickling waterfall of Magic Water cascading down the side
running into a foaming stream where
he fly-fished as a kid in Colorado.

We talked about the rickety wooden bridge he built across the gorge
that leads into the other cliff face beyond the orchard
and how he was troubleshooting for days to figure out
just why his Chattanooga would derail on exiting the far tunnel —
he took apart the track, cleaned it, rubbed it, resoldered the connectors —
the switch is jammed, or there must be plaster caught in the ties, he shrugged.

He talked on and on about his old Baltimore & Ohio steam locomotive
whose stack still billows wisps of actual smoke,
if you pop off its golden whistle and squeeze down some drops,
but whose motor is now too gummed up to churn.

He talked till I stood on the caboose railing next to him, watching the
granite cliffside fade back,
the track slinking beneath us under a wake of smoke,
the thundering wheels and the occasional bell,
till he leaned forward and shook my hand firmly,
"It's okay, doctor. I know it's spread,"
and we talked some more about everything but.

———

*Majid Mohiuddin, thirty-six, is a radiation oncologist in the Chicago-land area.
His poem is based on conversations with three patients whose similar perspectives
helped shape the narrative. It was first published in the* Canadian Medical
Association Journal *in June 2012.*

An earlier poem, "The Diagnosis," was included in The Cancer Poetry
Project, *volume one. While that poem focused on a doctor delivering bad news
to a patient, this poem has the doctor on the receiving end of a patient's news.*

Mohiuddin also has writings in the Journal of General Internal Medicine,
The Pharos, Brown Alumni Magazine, Modern Bride, Voices: Best Essays in
Publications *(anthology), and* An Audience of One, *his own poetry book of
English ghazals.*

*Mohiuddin previously practiced in academia in Baltimore and in private
practice in Houston. He trained at Brown and Harvard University, where he
was introduced to the use of literature and creative writing to help patients find
their own voice and initiate emotional healing.*

WAITING FOR POST-OP LAB RESULTS

by Terry S. Johnson

She tossed all night, her dreams
descending to a hell of horrible
possibility. Her cancer growing
deep roots, gnarled into organs,
cells too thick and twisted to be
eradicated by even the most
aggressive of medical arsenals.
She's not yet tired of fighting,
but knows that a time may come
when she raises the white flag,
conquered, or better yet, walks
into battle wearing a bull's eye,
larger than the wire mesh used
for radiation. She'll politely
invite the fatal intrusion, so weary
will she be of all the rigamarole.

As she is driven to the hospital
the next day, she's contained
in a kind of hysterical silence,
an implosion of sorts. She wonders
if she might spontaneously combust
like a Dicken's character she read
about in college. Now the tunnel
traffic is terrible, the valets all busy,
every wheelchair occupied. Shuffling
to the surgeon's office, she almost
doesn't care what he will say, so worn
out is she by this small effort. She longs
to go back to bed, enjoy the fresh air
in her bedroom. This November
morning was strangely beautiful
and she left all her windows open.

Terry S. Johnson, sixty-three, wrote this poem while helping her best friend, Jane, recover from her third melanoma surgery in twelve years. Jane has already survived ovarian cancer thirty years ago. Johnson wrote the poem to demonstrate the feelings of both strength and vulnerability that co-exist in the heart and mind of a cancer patient.

Johnson recently received her Master of Fine Arts degree in Writing from the Vermont College of Fine Arts. She has published in the Peregrine, *the* Berkshire Review, *the* New Verse News, *and other publications.*

Johnson is a retired sixth-grade school teacher and lives in Northampton, Massachusetts. Now that her two children are grown and prospering, she ditched her "soccer mom" van for a hybrid and enjoys yoga, foreign films, reading, and daily writing.

WARRIOR

by Carol Allis

She strips off her top
with the casualness of one
grown accustomed to her barrenness,
apologizes briefly, though she knows she doesn't need to
and exposes her blank chest with a single seam across the middle,
a terse reminder of a brush with death
(and death lost, temporarily),
her "courageous battle with cancer" as the obits say.
The flatness of her chest is a statement:
Here I am — take it or leave it — I'm fine with it,
stripped of the one thing
all women seem defined by.
I am a living, breathing icon
of wholeness.
I have lost what is falsely most prized
and — surprise — am still a human being.
No, more than that.
I am a walking soul, a triumph
of mind over matter,
a survivor
and the epitome of who we really are,
we women,
heart and soul and brain.
Look at me — look at who I am
without the breastplate
that is supposed to define me.
I have stronger armor
than you think

Just see what I can do…

Carol Allis, sixty-six, was inspired to write this poem by the cancer experiences of many loved ones. "The poem is dedicated to all of them, but in particular, to a friend who was diagnosed more than twenty years ago. She is alive and well, as are my beloved daughter-in-law and several other friends who have had breast cancer."

Allis says she's had "a special vendetta against cancer" since her mother died of lung cancer nearly twenty-five years ago. "I can't fight it with much money or medicine, but I will fight it with hope, support and love — and poetry." Her first book of poetry is Poems for Ordinary People. *Her poems have also appeared in the* North Coast Review.

Allis lives in Minnetonka, Minnesota, "close to beloved family." She has been writing since she was seven when her father gave her a manual Underwood typewriter. She has written professionally for decades and currently writes news for Hennepin County.

THE WAY HORSES ARE

by Larry Schug

He was silent for a moment,
then came back on the line,
a catch in his voice.
He said his horse,
standing at the corral fence,
had been looking toward the house
since early this morning.
He's looking for me, he said,
he doesn't understand cancer,
or that I don't have the strength
to go out and feed him, brush him,
scratch his ears,
hold a carrot to his soft lips.
He choked up again, said
that horse would wait for him
'til the end of its days,
unaware he'd reached the end of his.
That's just the way horses are.

My friend can't see me,
but I'm standing beside that horse
and I'll be looking for him
until the end of my days, too,
wishing we could talk once more.
That's just the way friends are.

"'The Way Horses Are' practically wrote itself after my last phone conversation with Roger," says Larry Schug, sixty-five, of his friend who died of colon cancer. "Fortunately, I was able to visit him once more at his house on the Prairie River in northern Minnesota. He died the next day." Roger, he says, loved the outdoors and built his house from logs on his property. He also loved horses, especially his horse, Laddie. He left behind his wife, two daughters, and a son.

Schug has often written poetry about loved ones' experiences with cancer. "I feel it's my job, my duty, as a poet to remember these people," he says. "As a human being, I just couldn't let these people go without somehow memorializing them. I loved them all and miss them greatly." Schug has written six books of poems, the latest being Nails. His poems have been included in many print and online publications.

Schug is retired from the College of St. Benedict, where he worked for thirty-four years. He lives with his wife, dog, and three cats near a beautiful tamarack bog in St. Wendel Township, Minnesota. He volunteers at the Writing Center at St. Ben's and as a naturalist at the arboretum at St. John's University in Collegeville, Minnesota.

YOU WERE

By Autumn Stephens

"won't be there tomorrow," you said
six months ricocheted in your brain and, god,
what you wouldn't have given for one solid night of sleep
but what if

"won't be there," you said
but in the end, you made your customary
grand entrance into our motley survivors' circle
the queen's smile on your rouged lips your back a rigid
wooden ruler

you conjured Elizabeth I that autumn morning
ruffed and wrinkled   strong as god and as fierce
as Shirley MacLaine   a dancer's discipline
the show that must always go on

so when you said no tears, we sucked up our salt
lest our blue-ink memories drown on the page
a marbled swirl, gibberish in a runaway sea

that was the day you wrote of the blazing orange season
pumpkins   hungry ghosts   the opposite of water
your greedy run-on sentences unreeling across acres
of paper stabbed through with dashes and dependent clauses
as though you could not bear to bring them to an end —

come December, enormous forget-me-nots would bloom
in your fading face, eyes of Julie Christie in love in snow
or the lost princess Anastasia doomed by her own blood

but now in high harvest you held court in linen robes
backlit by the cresting sun, and your gaze glinted like sparks
from crossed sabers
"won't be there tomorrow," you said
but you were there, you were

---

*Autumn Stephens, fifty-six, is a breast cancer survivor and a healing writing
workshop facilitator, "helping cancer survivors heal through writing." Stephens
wrote "You Were" for Irene Bronston, a member of her writing group who died
of sarcoma. Stephens calls her smart, sassy, and "a citizen of the world."*

*"I vividly remember the October day she announced to the workshop
members that her doctors had run out of options — how the sun streamed
through the plate glass window, how Irene sternly instructed us not to cry.
By mid-April, she was dead."*

*Stephens' writings have appeared in myriad publications and anthologies,
including* Feisty First Ladies and Other Unforgettable White House
Women; The Secret Lives of Lawfully Wedded Wives: 27 Women Writers
on Love, Infidelity, Sex Roles, Race, Kids, and More; *and* Roar Softly and
Carry a Great Lipstick: 28 Women Writers on Life, Sex, and Survival.

WRITING POETRY: HOW TO GET STARTED

Perhaps you've been browsing through this book, reading the poems that fill its pages. Maybe some of the words and images have touched you unexpectedly. "Blah, Blah, Blah, Cancer" (page 137) isn't a likely way to begin a poem, but it catches our attention with the first word — exactly the perfect word—and pulls us into the poem. Or perhaps you were drawn to "Posted Notice for Pileated Woodpecker" (page 49) for its quirky humor or "Playing in the Band" for its happy exuberance (page 246).

Maybe some poems have brought tears to your eyes. Others may have compelled you to read them twice or three times. Some may have said just what you have wanted to say or voiced just how you feel.

If reading others' poems has moved you to pick up a pencil — or your laptop — and write your own poetry, offered here are some tips that may help you get started.

This type of poetry may be new to you — poems that don't rhyme and/or don't often fit into patterns, as did the singsong rhymes we learned as kids. Every poet in this book searched for just the right words to bring clarity and depth of feeling to their poems and to us, their readers.

All of us, adults and children, have poems inside us. In classrooms, I've often found that the child who is the saddest or the loneliest — the one for whom life is most difficult — writes the most amazing or surprising poems. The language of poetry seems to have been born in them, and once they comprehend its power and the satisfaction of writing their own experiences, they create poems that speak to us.

Similarly, adults who are suffering and/or dealing with pain, fear, or grief — or joy and excitement — write poems like those found in this second volume of *The Cancer Poetry Project*.

Some poems, like "Breathing" (page 13), were written by people who never had written poetry before. Other poems were written by award-winning poets. Most poets in the book fall somewhere in between these experiences.

When the invitation to submit poems for this book went out, some poets wrote special poems to participate; others sent in poems previously published in literary journals; and still others found poems in desks or notebooks that had lain there, just waiting for the right time of discovery. Jennifer Freed, who submitted "Yet There Is Still Such Beauty" (page 199), wrote, "Until now my poems have only lived in my notebooks." Now her poem lives in this book.

Where do poems come from? Lucille Clifton, a leading U.S. poet, says of poetry, "Poetry began when somebody walked off a savanna or out of a cave and looked up at the sky with wonder and said, 'Ah-h-h!' That was the first poem."

Sometimes a poem grows slowly, word by word, until it is whole. Other times, a poem takes over our fingers as we write quickly to capture the words that are flying through our minds.

A fourth-grade student, writing poetry with me in her classroom, said, "When I write a poem, my pencil feels like a cloud racing across the paper, and I have no control over it." Rarely can we write a poem on command. As this student said, it comes from inside the writer — rarely as a response to a directive.

What purpose does poetry serve? I believe that poetry lets us know that we are not alone, that others feel what we feel. If a tender poem brings you to tears, perhaps the person who wrote the poem cried too while writing it. We can find comfort in the words of a poem and in the reading of it, either silently or aloud. Writing a joyous poem, and reading it, either to oneself or in the company of others, is a celebration of words and feelings.

If you are a poet, then at sometime, somewhere, you have seen and heard the language of poetry and have hungered for it yourself. When I was eleven, I met a wonderful poet who spent most of her life confined to a wheelchair. I loved being with her. She was, my mother whispered, a *poet*. What a wonderful thing to be! Her poems made me want to be a poet too. She wrote of her yearly wait for spring to come, and her poems made me aware of how this special language speaks to us, calls to us.

How do you begin? Simply *start*. Read the poems in *The Cancer Poetry Project* or browse in libraries and bookstores to find poetry you like — poems written by men, women, and children; the young and the old; mechanics, gardeners, and attorneys; musicians and scientists. These poems are like jumper cables, helping us learn the language of poetry and suggesting ways to join in.

- Now get writing, but keep it simple. Use powerful, strong words.
- Read your poetry aloud as you write it. Tune your ears to listen: does it sound *right*?

- Consider using repetition, as Pamela Manché Pearce uses in "My TV Family" (page 101): "I sit in the big house in the big chair and watch the big TV." Or Sara Torrey's "Elegy for That Girl in the Polka Dot Bra" (page 16): "… bald, bald like an old man bald, bald like an eagle bald, like an egg."
- The power of a poem is often found in the last line, as in Kelina Leeks' "In the Other Room" (page 31): "…when I am gone." Consider packing your own last line with power.
- Share your poems and remember that they belong to you. No one can say that your poem is *wrong*; it is yours to write and to share as you wish.

There is an explosion of poetry happening all over our country. Poetry readings are held in big cities and small towns alike, in restaurants and coffeehouses, bookstores and churches. People gather to share what is in their poets' hearts. Many of these individuals are, for the first time, finding their voices, saying what is inside them. It may be the best way, the only way, to say who they really are. Poetry is how we speak when no other way of speaking will do.

And now… get writing. It's your turn.

Joy C. Bumgardner is a poet, an author, and a retired educator. She supplied invaluable editorial help in crafting both volumes of The Cancer Poetry Project. *She has authored three writing books, including* Helping Students Learn to Write, Helping Students Learn to Write Poetry, *and* My Writing Book; *two children's books,* The Magic Donkey *and* The Marvelous Monster; *and numerous stories and poems for children's magazines.*

Bumgardner is the mother of three children and the grandmother of nine grandchildren. She and her husband of fifty-three years, Larry, live in Plymouth, Minnesota.

Acknowledgement for previously published works:

- "After the 34th MRI" by Geo Staley, first published in *Ready for Any Nuance* (Finishing Line Press, 2011).
- "After the Diagnosis" by Annette Opalczynski, first published in *The Sun,* August 2007.
- "Cancer, for Dickie" by Cathy Barber, first published in *The Bohemian,* Notre Dame de Namur University, 2006–2007.
- "Chayote Fruit" by Kyle Potvin, first published in *Sound Travels on Water* (Finishing Line Press, 2012).
- "Fed-Ex" by Clinton B. Campbell, first published in *A String of Colored Beads,* New Jersey Poetry Society Anthology, 2006.
- "Hymn to a Lost Breast" by Bonnie Maurer, first published in *The Reconfigured Goddess: Poems of a Breast Cancer Survivor* (Finishing Line Press, 2013).
- "Infusion Fridays" by Terry Godbey, first published in *The Florida Review,* 2012.
- "Kitty Smiled" by Gary Young, first published in *Braver Deeds* (Gibbs Smith, 1999), winner of the Peregrine Smith Poetry Prize.
- "Leaving the Clinic" by Marilyn L. Taylor, first published in the *Journal of the American Medical Association,* 279, No. 22 (June 10, 1998).
- "Miracles" by Paul Hostovsky, first published in *A Little in Love a Lot* (Main Street Rag, 2011).
- "Night at the Opera" by Marc Straus, first published in *Not God: A Play in Verse* (Northwestern University Press, 2006).
- "On the Day of Her Diagnosis" by Barbara Crooker, first published in *Dogwood,* Volume 6, Spring 2006.
- "Posted Notice for Pileated Woodpecker" by Laura L. Snyder, first published in *Classifieds: An Anthology of Prose Poems* (Equinox Publishing, 2012).
- "Right to Life" by Patti Marschock, first published in *The Morpo Review,* Volume 12, Issue 1 (November 12, 2006).
- "Sanctuary" by Meredith Davies Hadaway, first published in *Fishing Secrets of the Dead* (Word Press, 2005).
- "Shaving Our Heads" by Gail Rudd Entrekin, first published in *Rearrangement of the Invisible* (Poetic Matrix Press, 2012).
- "Sloan Kettering" by Lynn Mayson Shapiro, first published in *Pushcart Prize, XXXII: Best of the Small Presses,* 2008 Edition.
- "Sweetie, Sweetie" by Margot Wizansky, first published in *Antigonish Review.*
- "This Camp" by Leonore M. Montanaro, first published in *The Morning Within the Dark* (Montanaro Press, 2012).
- "Trainspotting in the Clinic" by Majid Mohiuddin, first published in *Canadian Medical Association Journal,* June 12, 2012.
- "Uncovered" by Cynthia Rausch Allar, first published on the Winning Writers website, third-place winner of the Margaret Reid Poetry Contest (2007).
- "Warrior" by Carol Allis, first published in *Poems for Ordinary People* (North Star Press, 2012).